Empowerment and Innovation

Managers, Principles and Reflective Practice

Martin Beirne

Senior Lecturer in Organisational Behaviour,
School of Business and Management,
University of Glasgow
Scotland, UK

Edward Elgar
Cheltenham, UK • Northampton, MA, USA

Published by
Edward Elgar Publishing Limited
Glensanda House
Montpellier Parade
Cheltenham
Glos GL50 1UA
UK

Edward Elgar Publishing, Inc.
William Pratt House
9 Dewey Court
Northampton
Massachusetts 01060
USA

Paperback edition 2007

A catalogue record for this book
is available from the British Library

Library of Congress Cataloguing in Publication Data

Beirne, Martin, 1960-
    Empowerment and Innovation : managers, principles and reflective practice /
Martin Beirne.
        p. cm.
    Includes bibliographical references and index.
        1. Management–Employee participation–Great Britain. I. Title.

HD5660.G7B45 2006
658.3'1520941–dc22
                                                                2005052797

ISBN: 978 1 84376 246 1 (cased)
ISBN: 978 1 84720 499 8 (paperback)

Printed by Biddles Ltd, King's Lynn, Norfolk

Empowerment and Innovation

For Sean and Leigh
and
to the memory of Harvie Ramsay

Contents

Foreword

This book aims to engage the interest of two constituencies. In career terms, the first operates at the sharp end of management and organisation, in the practical world of affairs. This is an audience of prospective and practising managers, or, more specifically, people within this category who are favourably disposed towards employee empowerment, who articulate at least some commitment to the value of grassroots decision-taking, and who would do something positive to enact direct participation within their own situations. Although they represent the traditional target market for consultants and suppliers of prescriptive advice, these tend to be people who, through experience or involvement in management education, remain uneasy about the quality of the material that speaks directly to their concerns. Many of the readers in this category will, I'm sure, have encountered trite and unhelpful pronouncements and opportunistic interventions that draw a veil over the problems and issues that affect their practice. Some will have been disappointed or frustrated by 'how to do it' techniques that are poorly grounded in the realities and dilemmas of organisational life. Collectively, this population is looking for more telling and potent management knowledge that can help them to make a difference in their working lives.

The people in our second constituency, namely critical social scientists and management commentators, provide the intellectual weight to support these everyday concerns, reinforcing the sense of inadequacy with prescriptive accounts of empowerment and participation. One of the most encouraging features of the past decade or so has been the dramatic expansion of work within the critical tradition of management studies that challenges the simplistic images and ideas traded in this area. As we shall see, social researchers are highly critical of a whole range of supposedly empowering initiatives, highlighting a contrast between rhetoric and substance, presenting rich empirical studies and offering a detailed analysis of contextualising influences and constraints. The net result is a much stronger research base from which to explore the practical possibilities for empowerment. Yet this material is rarely absorbed into practitioner debates or followed through to agenda discussions that might assist front-line enthusiasts. Indeed, the findings of critical research regularly miss a practitioner audience, a situation that is largely attributable to the propensity of the research community to remain aloof.

Too many critical commentators unfortunately adopt an abstentionist position on practice, cutting their analyses short, stopping with the empirical results of their investigations, or demolishing guru prescriptions without considering the practical, organisational implications of their conclusions. Their work is loaded towards the early stages of what might usefully be called the full cycle of research. The major preoccupations, and indeed achievements, have been analytical and empirical, advancing our conceptual understanding of empowerment. Yet the momentum tends to stop at this point. The focus is almost exclusively on analysis and explanation, at the expense of following through to an explicit logic of practice. This dimension is conceded, by default, to consultants and prescriptive commentators who seem more interested or adept at engaging with practitioners, despite the negative reactions they often elicit. Even when attention is given to negative or unpalatable aspects of empowerment, the concern that critical writers demonstrate for staff on the receiving end is rarely matched by applied knowledge that can speak to those in the position, or with the inclination, to do something about it, to those who would become activists for change.

Some social scientists compound the access difficulty for managers by adopting a purist stance in their work, limiting their role to exploring ideals and articulating their sense of what ought to be in an ideal world, rather than addressing thorny issues of development. This is an understandable, if disappointing, position when so many research studies legitimately give rise to considerable pessimism about the obstacles to progress. For others, however, the flight from practical thinking is defensive and career-minded, rather than utopian.

Following the full research cycle from theoretical and investigative work to a consistent logic of practice is certainly fraught with difficulties. Generations of social scientists have issued warnings about the dangers of dual role compromises and the perils of dealing with practitioners. Eldridge (1980) provides a notable example with the call for researchers who would be relevant to beware. The gist of his argument is, quite rightly, that the challenge of being relevant often has strings attached. Recipients usually expect relevant research to be congenial rather than critical, useful on their own terms, otherwise it becomes unacceptable or threatening. This raises the spectre of conservatism that has long haunted the human relations tradition of management research, and which critical writers are determined to avoid. Hence, there are justifiable worries about 'managerialising the debate' (Thompson, 1986), or somehow encouraging the misappropriation of critical knowledge by enthusiasts for authoritarianism and tight labour control (Nord and Jermier, 1992).

Of course, the dangers of slippage from, or misappropriation of, progressive ideas are very real. However, it seems that there is also a thin line between caution and negativity. It can be easier and safer for critical commentators to rail against the prescriptive pronouncement of gurus and consultants, and to underscore the limited or tentative results of empowerment schemes, than extend their work to the challenge of managing and realising change. Unhappily, social scientists can risk their research credentials in the realm of practice and open themselves to the charge of becoming ideologically unsound, possibilities that offer a powerful disincentive to applied work.

This is where we find the less excusable and debilitating side of critical management studies. Some contributions seem to equate the critical approach with an anti-management position, or are least their style can generate that perception among management readers. A deeply ingrained sense of 'them and us' feeds an oppositional stance in at least part of the critical literature, which aligns itself unambiguously with employee interests while presenting managers as the unquestioning and unitary agents of workplace misery. Mandel (1973) provides an obvious example, rejecting any link between contemporary management and progressive practice. His is not an abstentionist but a rejectionist position, saddling managers with an essential interest in labour control and dismissing empowerment as a means of concealing potential disagreements with staff.

Others produce negative assessments without such a rigidly servile image of managers. Hales (2000) provides a recent example, giving the impression, intentional or otherwise, that particular categories of middle and junior managers are against empowerment, or play calculating games with it to defend their own status and personal interests. This is theoretically positive insofar as it acknowledges the scope for managerial agency and choice, yet by reducing this to career politics and financial interests it reinforces the narrow, calculating and unhelpful image of management that survives within critical social research.

We are now at a point in history when people from a wide range of backgrounds, and with all sorts of personal values and beliefs, are employed under one management label or another. Some will have good reason to be worried about their jobs and to think defensively about their reactions to empowerment, especially where employers connect it with de-layering and downsizing policies. Yet management behaviour is not reducible to self-interest alone. For this category of humanity, as for any other, thoughts about personal advantage or disadvantage are cross-cut by ethical considerations and various social values.

Contrary to the sentiments expressed by some critical writers, there are practising and aspiring managers who baulk at the traditions of tight labour control within modern organisations. There are managers who identify with critical writings and articulate a genuine concern for principles of fairness, justice and direct participation. Certainly, there are students in management education that would benefit from research that can lead to firmer views about how they can 'make a difference', how they can enact serious concerns and remain faithful to expressed values as they seek a living in management positions. More experienced hands can also be expected to benefit, empirical research indicating that personal concepts of self, integrity and morality continue to burn in managers throughout their careers, often adding a sense of struggle and dissatisfaction as they deal with everyday pressures and heartfelt contradictions (Watson, 1994).

Even if the suspicion remains that empowerment is somehow compromised or loaded towards employer interests, critical commentators could be more sensitive to the predicament of front-line managers who share a positive outlook. There could be more of an effort to acknowledge variability in the underlying values that move practitioners, and to relate this to a sense of management activism that might sustain progressive inclinations. This would enable the research community to reach beyond traditional debates and client groups, giving researchers the opportunity to apply their knowledge of organisational dilemmas and constraints, and to anticipate alternative possibilities, rather than occasionally wringing their hands about problems and poor experiences.

Initial pointers towards an applied research agenda have already been provided, albeit rather tentatively, by critical researchers who have taken employment in business school environments, and find that the issue has been forced for them as teachers of managers, especially on MBA and related programmes. Collins (2000) and Goulding and Currie (2000) provide examples of work that aims to package critical thinking and empirical research for a wider audience in management education, and to cultivate a more analytical and reflective practice. Using the phraseology adopted by Collins, this is 'critical-practical' in the sense of engaging with actors who may be committed to empowerment (Collins, 2000, p. 247) yet susceptible to technician thinking and the ill-conceived prescriptions of gurus and consultants.

As part of a broader attempt to inculcate the habits of critical scrutiny and promote active reflection, this line of development can be extremely useful, encouraging managers to 'stand back' from everyday pressures and question their attitudes, resources, activities and associations. However, it amounts to a partial and underdeveloped tendency, falling short of the effort needed to complete the full cycle of research.

In fact, some of the critical material that has emerged on reflective practice is disappointing, failing to match expressed aims with substantive content, and offering little more than a new spin on the old argument that 'there is nothing so practical as a good theory'. This is surely an accurate dictum when theoretical knowledge prompts an informed understanding of issues and an ability to interpret the problematics of empowerment, rendering practitioners less vulnerable to the toolkit views of consultants and the packaged accompaniments to passive management education. Yet the emphasis is still on a prior stage to action. What the researchers are aiming to provide is a sensitising experience, equipping people with a greater ability to think and to play their own part in organisations as their awareness of conditions and constraints develops. The participants are then left to their own devices, to make their own sense of critical research and, more importantly, to find their own way of translating critical capabilities into a consistent practice. This is a truncated form of critical management studies.

Encouraging managers to reflect upon the principles and implications of their engagement with employees is only part of what is involved in pursuing the full cycle of critical research. Anticipating new possibilities and enlarging the collective stock of knowledge about alternative options is a neglected part of the agenda. Some of the most influential social scientists of the past half-century, including Tom Burns (1967), C. Wright Mills (1973) and Richard Brown (1984), have argued along similar lines that questioning, theorising and reflecting should be positively linked to the search for better ways of organising and managing:

> Thus it seems to me that an essential part of our task is to question and to investigate alternatives – activities which may often be combined...few, if any, of us who try to find out and understand what work is like in our society will feel that there is no room for improvement; and exploring the conditions which make possible situations as they are is also, at least implicitly, to begin to establish how they might be different (Brown, 1984, p. 317).

> The purpose of sociology is to achieve an understanding of social behaviour and social institutions which is different from that current among the people through whose conduct institutions exist, an understanding which is not merely different but new and better. The practice of sociology is criticism...It is the business of sociologists to conduct a critical debate with the public about its equipment of social institutions (Burns, 1967, pp. 366-7).

For these figures, it is a matter of professional responsibility that critical commentators enact the full research cycle and 'follow through' on the practicalities of progressive management. This means ranging beyond theoretical conventions, the rules of evidence and sensitive reflection, in this case relating critical reviews of empowerment to envisaging and programme building activities that have practical merit.

This book makes a deliberate attempt to apply critical research to the problematic of enacting and sustaining direct participation, and to the challenge of addressing managers who would give practical meaning to the concept of employee empowerment. It is written polemically, as well as academically, to stimulate creative thinking about the everyday meaning of principled and reflective management, and the prospects for channelling research on the 'working out' of participation schemes into applied knowledge that can inform a progressive practice in the 'here and now'. This is an attempt to frame possibilities for innovative management without slipping to unrealistic or utopian assumptions.

There is a significant degree of correspondence between this approach and transformative projects in engineering and computing innovation, where critiques of orthodox prescriptions and standard ways of organising and managing development work have paved the way to innovative possibilities and very practical alternatives. Theorist practitioners such as Cooley (1980) and Rosenbrock (1990), and computing scientists in the participatory design community (Greenbaum and Kyng, 1991), have made a point of 'getting their hands dirty', of contemplating, devising, enacting, testing and evaluating new possibilities. Echoing the sentiments of Burns and Brown, they conceive their role as not merely adding to the stock of available knowledge, but as challenging conventional ideas and finding ways to increase the congruence between empowering values and everyday job performance.

Drawing inspiration from this material, as well as telling episodes from empowerment initiatives in other contexts, critical research will be connected to three levels of practical engagement. The first concentrates on the linkage to scrutinising, thinking and reflecting, building upon the emerging tendency to cultivate analytical and interpretive capabilities through critical management studies. However, it will add focus and specificity to established images of "critical-practical" knowledge (Collins, 2000) by mapping essential characteristics and qualities that can enhance reflective thinking about empowerment. These will be summarised in the penultimate chapter, although from the earliest stages empirical research will be harnessed to flag some of the issues, difficulties and dilemmas bearing upon practical initiatives, so that enthusiasts are better equipped to apply judgemental and interpretive abilities in favour of empowerment in their own settings.

Shifting the emphasis from thinking to doing, the second level of practice considers engaging and enacting activities, recalling Pateman's (1970) attention to participatory competence and the learned capacity to overcome obstacles and inhibitions. Recognising the managerial challenge of aligning principles and ambitions with situated learning and sustainable collaboration, down-to-earth guidance about what helps and hinders will be drawn from the case material assembled through the early chapters, and by introducing insights from research on community theatre. The latter is instructive because community theatre practitioners are also de facto managers. Their role is to help members of the public to engage in the creative process of producing involving drama or delivering theatre that connects with local issues and speaks to local concerns. This means co-ordinating and enabling participants from a wide range of situations and predicaments (including young offenders, retired people, disabled and handicapped groups and residents of housing estates, among many others) to reach their full potential and express their views in a telling and effective manner. The precariousness of empowerment can be very obvious in this context, hence practitioners tend to have a heightened sense of the intimacy between sensitive reflection and management activism. Their experience in moving between these dimensions, together with their accumulated knowledge of creative possibilities for engagement, have much wider applicability, bringing options for negotiating progress and sustaining empowerment more sharply into focus.

Finally, attention turns to public policy and questions about the regulatory framework within which voluntary commitments to empowerment are articulated. State and supra state initiatives will be evaluated in terms of their enabling or constraining effects on local attempts to enact empowerment. The effectiveness of the relevant social provisions of the European Union will be a prominent consideration, though in pursuing the full cycle of research the analysis will extend into the developmental aspects of building and refining framework initiatives that are conducive to progressive management at the grassroots.

Acknowledgements

Many of the arguments and ideas presented in this book were rehearsed at various conferences, seminars and workshops during the last few years. They have been developed, clarified and sharpened as a result of the responses offered and feedback received, as colleagues and participants will hopefully recognise. I would offer my grateful thanks to all concerned.

My sense of the possibilities for an empowering management practice has been greatly enhanced by the experience of conducting collaborative research with Stephanie Knight. Her creative energy, boundless enthusiasm and fearless sincerity have had a major impact on my outlook and direction.

My interest in practice, and conviction that critical research should have something valuable to say to practitioners, to people outside of academia, is largely due to the influence of my local community and close circle of friends. The relevance of research for front-line people in the Clyde shipyards, in silicon valley electronics plants, the civil engineering industry and local authorities has been a consistent talking point for a large number of years. I've heard plenty of disparaging comments, most of them humorous yet some of them telling as these managers and workers bear little resemblance to the images of themselves that often appear in the literature.

This book is dedicated jointly to my children, Sean and Leigh, and to the memory of Harvie Ramsay. Harvie's impact on my life, as tutor, colleague and collaborator, has been profound. I'm not at all sure if he would approve of the more optimistic images of practice that appear in this book. However, his influence continues to burn as I struggle to pursue the standards of clarity and analytical rigour that he represented.

Finally, thanks are due to Kirsteen Wilson for her technical wizardry in formatting this book, and for skilfully defending space and time for my writing.

Martin Beirne
May 2005

1. Anticipating a new era of consensus management?

This is a book about one of the most celebrated and controversial business subjects of recent years: employee empowerment and direct participation in the governance and management of modern organisations. Widely touted as key organising principles for private companies, the public sector and even not-for-profit organisations, the twin themes of empowerment and participation have been deployed both as worthy innovations in their own right and as indispensable features of broader movements and tendencies, including total quality management (Robson, 1988; Dean and Evans, 1994) and business process re-engineering (Hammer and Champy, 1993). To believe some of the populist and promotional material now available, empowerment is a new management philosophy, the central concept in progressive thinking about business and management, and something that credible executives must be seen to endorse on a regular basis (see Hales, 2000; Collins 2000). However, when stripped of the spin and the public relations hoopla that now surrounds the topic, empowerment is essentially about collective influence and the sharing of knowledge, insight and experience to improve organisational performance.

Much of the interest in empowerment is pragmatic, related not to managerial consumerism or fashionable ideology but to its market potential. Since the 1980s, influential management writers have supported empowerment as a practical matter of good business. Prominent Americans such as Tom Peters (1987) and Rosabeth Kanter (1984) prepared the ground for a large number of contemporary commentators who take a hard line against hierarchical approaches to controlling employees and limiting their discretion, arguing that these are anachronistic in a fast-moving and complex competitive environment (Foy, 1994; Caudron, 1995; Khan, 1997; Roth, 1997; Ward, 1996). The competitive challenges of thriving in global markets and harnessing rapidly changing technologies put a premium on responsiveness, flexibility and imagination throughout organisations, qualities that are stifled rather than cultivated by rigid job structures and the strict demarcation of tasks and responsibilities. From here, empowerment is a matter of straightforward economics, of acknowledging the potential value in untapped human resources and the folly of restricting access to these by following outmoded practices in a changing world.

This economic rationale can also be heard in public policy debates, where empowerment is now cast within a wider modernising agenda to boost employment and promote economic regeneration. However, in this realm it becomes entangled with other labels, such as partnership, social inclusion and lifelong learning. Although used frequently and together, these terms are not synonymous, and offer an initial indication of the elastic phraseology and contrasting meanings that are attached to this subject.

For the member states of the European Union, and for the British government, the economic aspects of empowerment are interrelated with principles of fairness and consensus (Commission of the European Union, 1998; Department of Trade and Industry, 1999). Crucial attention is given to developing the citizen and the community as well as the economy. This looks beyond the employability and adaptability of individuals to various concerns about their quality of working life. A humanist dimension is added, extending the reach of empowerment and recalling the earliest references to the term, as a way of helping handicapped and disabled people to assert themselves and exert an independent influence on their situations (Heller, 1999). Employers are encouraged to provide arrangements that nurture autonomy and personal growth, increasing the scope for self-determination at the workplace and reducing the formal dependence on managerial directives. The other partners in the employment relationship, the employees and their representatives in trade unions and other associations, are persuaded of the merits of consensual labour relations and of maintaining collaborative ties for mutual advantage.

Extending this concern for the career situation of employees and their wider role as citizens, some accounts cast the net even further, presenting empowerment as a democratising process that can counteract feelings of political marginalisation (notably Bachrach and Botwinick, 1992). Recalling British debates on industrial democracy from the 1970s (Burns and Doyle, 1981; Brannen et al., 1976; Poole, 1986), much of the interest here is on enfranchising workers into forms of organisational citizenship that permit collective decision-making about policy and strategy as well as operational matters. However, in contemporary accounts, the connection between local and national levels of political participation is attracting greater attention, prompted by very basic worries about the decline and decay of democratic institutions.

The linkage between workplace and polity that informs this broader vision of empowerment has itself been investigated by a long tradition of social scientists, variously emphasising the benefits of grassroots industrial decision-making for social learning, collective awareness and even public spiritedness (Pateman, 1970). Blumberg (1968, p. 109) captures the essence of this with a line that has been regularly cited through the last three decades:

'The organisation that permits participation ultimately produces individuals who are responsible to participate.' Active industrial citizenship ostensibly carries broader advantages, promoting a greater sense of social responsibility, democratic competence and a willingness to participate in the democratic institutions of civil society. Against a background of rising public cynicism and political apathy in Britain, the United States and elsewhere, this political vision of employee empowerment is gaining fresh impetus.

The symptoms of faltering democracy have been well documented, with a persistent decline in voting populations and hostile reactions to political spin and scandal. In Britain, despite the historic significance of devolution and the creation of a Scottish Parliament, large numbers of people are opting out of the democratic process (Wood, 1999). In Scotland, as in other countries, the turnout for voting at local and national elections has fallen to around 50 per cent, a figure that has also been applied to participation rates in the rest of Britain and in the United States (by Bachrach and Botwinick, 1992, among others). For all the hope of an enlivened democratic impulse via devolved government, almost half of the population is not moved to participate.

With this backdrop to the expanding discussion of empowerment at the workplace, it is hardly surprising that social scientists should revisit earlier debates and consider empowerment as a political phenomenon. For political theorists such as Bachrach and Botwinick (1992), empowerment commands attention for its democratic possibilities, as a means of reinvigorating citizens in their employment and, by extension, revitalising national institutions. Empowerment becomes an enabling mechanism, not just for economic or commercial advantage but for political development, as a means of boosting transferable skills and inclinations that can be carried over to the civic domain.

Of course, this takes empowerment on a conceptual journey that ranges well beyond the initial preoccupations of management writers, opening controversial issues, notably the defence of managerial prerogatives and the legitimacy of collective decision-making on key areas of business activity. Historically, references to democracy have sparked a variety of conflicting impulses and emotions, negative and indifferent as well as positive, from people who feel threatened more than liberated, and from some who detect little more than spin in the latest round of fashionable phraseology. Despite its current approval rating, the essence of what is considered to be empowerment varies significantly in terms of the aims and ambitions that are attached to the topic and the conceptual underpinnings that produce contrasting evaluations of progress and practice. It is vital to acknowledge this level of complexity, not only to understand the reactions and tensions that can be generated by different pronouncements, but also to pursue a sensitive and consistent view of programmes and initiatives that claim to offer improvements of one sort or another.

Despite the thrust of a large business-focused literature, employee empowerment is not conceptually confined to the local and proximal level of the workplace or to matters of internal functioning. It is not reducible to the effectiveness of work technology or the influence that employees exert over their immediate task environment. Nor is it restricted to the economics of employment and global competitiveness. Empowerment is imbued with democratic credentials and concerns for social justice. It is politically correct in a number of different ways, as symbolic language for progressive management, as a way of encouraging personal growth and autonomy, as socially responsible corporate behaviour, and as a route to political maturity.

PRESCRIPTIVE IMAGES AND PRONOUNCEMENTS

The various meanings and ambitions that are attached to empowerment command attention, and often approval, because they seem to be at odds with the predominant principles of twentieth-century management and industrial organisation. Enthusiasts share a basic distaste for management orthodoxy and for traditional organisational structures that ostensibly weigh heavily on people, stifling their energy and enthusiasm and retarding human development, economically, socially or politically. This debilitating legacy is commonly associated with the ideology and apparatus of scientific management and the influence of Fordism in setting the terms on which jobs are usually designed and employee relations typically conducted.

The tendency over the past century has been for managers to take their cues from authoritarian ideas about good practice, operating with the assumption that workers are basically unreliable, troublesome or recalcitrant, requiring close supervision and disciplinary control to ensure any sort of consistent performance. These ideas were legitimised by Frederick Taylor with his pronouncements on scientific management (Taylor, 1911), and subsequently by Henry Ford who gave focus and force to their application with assembly line production methods (Ford and Crowther, 1926). Though originally developed at a time of expanding markets during the late nineteenth and early twentieth centuries, when the reorganisation of work on the shop-floor was considered to be a priority, the key to expanding output and satisfying demand, Taylorism and Fordism became pillars of orthodoxy, setting parameters for job design and for the conduct of labour relations through subsequent competitive conditions.

For Taylor and Ford, the fundamentals of management and organisation turned on the core problem of labour control. This was taken to be the most pressing business challenge of the epoch, and Taylor offered a view that appealed to many of his contemporaries. Workers were deliberately pursuing their own sectional interests, exploiting their crucial knowledge of production processes and engaging in 'systematic soldiering' to inflate wages by restricting output, thereby damaging profitability, especially under conditions of buoyant demand. His solution was to wrest control from the shop floor, to capture essential knowledge from communities of workers and systematically disempower them by separating conception from execution, disconnecting the thinking and 'doing' aspects of work. Management specialists would take over the conceptual dimension, planning and organising very detailed, non-discretionary and narrowly defined tasks that were to be the sole province of workers, with supervisors and overseers monitoring adherence and enforcing higher rates of productivity.

While Taylor applied his ideas to institutionalise control through tighter job structures in the American steel industry, it was Ford's mechanised regimentation and pacing of task performance that established hierarchical management and anti-employee involvement as mainstream features of organisational life. The assembly line became the engine of mass production as Ford's ideas about the simplification of car-making and the replacement of craft workers with cheaper sources of labour were taken up to service mass markets in other areas (Littler, 1985; Noon and Blyton, 1997). Consequently, the distinction between 'them and us', the 'two sides of industry', sharpened as the twentieth century progressed. Empowerment was conceptually reserved for management grades, at the expense of discretionary working on the shop floor and with knowledge that was previously concentrated in the minds of employees.

Despite the dramatic increases in output and productivity under Taylorist and Fordist regimes, and the corresponding distribution of goods and services to a wider population of consumers, there has always been an undercurrent of concern about the dehumanising impact on staff. The pressures of machine pacing and the difficulties of coping with narrow, tedious and repetitive jobs have taken a serious toll on the health and well-being of generations of workers, as numerous reports and humanistic critiques have demonstrated over the years (Sward, 1948; Beynon, 1973; Littler, 1985; Ciulla, 2000). They have also prompted responses and reactions that have been played out against a shifting backdrop of economic conditions, often demonstrating the limitations of tight control systems and adversarial labour relations.

Ford himself discovered that elaborate authoritarian structures can be counterproductive when buoyant labour markets enable people to 'vote with their feet', to find alternative employment and an escape from what they regard as unsatisfactory jobs. From the earliest stages of mass production, Ford and his followers in the car industry and beyond experienced recurring problems with labour turnover, absenteeism and conflict that mirrored the distinctive phases of the business cycle (Ford and Crowther, 1926; Littler, 1985). These often prompted an apparent softening of the regime and the provision of financial and other incentives to retain people in Taylorised jobs, including in Ford's case dramatic wage rises and socialisation programmes that aimed to induce a sense of commitment and duty to his company, especially among immigrant workers (Noon and Blyton, 1997).

Periods of high unemployment have typically been associated with the resurgence of authoritarian preoccupations, however, as in the late 1970s and early 1980s when recession effectively halted a movement to improve working conditions and reduce labour market problems. Many employers took this opportunity to restore command and control tactics, imposing wage cuts, extending working hours and intensifying job performance with little thought to the consequences for staff (Ciulla, 2000). Against the backdrop of unemployment and amid fears about job loss, they felt able to force through changes that would have been considered unacceptable or costly just a few years earlier.

Looking back on this particular period, many commentators are struck by the arrogance and myopia demonstrated by such employers. Influential management writers, including Tom Peters and Rosabeth Kanter, have pointed to the longer-term costs to companies that attempted to profit from economic coercion. Their approach was not only insensitive, it signalled an insularity and a failure to appreciate the changing nature of competition at a time when productivity was becoming less important as a source of business advantage than quality and flexibility. As markets became more turbulent, and manufacturers from the Pacific-rim captured ground from their Western counterparts by offering reliable and attractive products, Taylorised jobs and command structures looked increasingly anachronistic. Souring relations with disaffected workers seemed reckless. These people were central to the challenge of producing viable commodities for difficult markets. Yet the legacy of Taylorism and Fordism was stifling their capacity to care about what they produced or to seek improvements in products and processes by their own initiative. The lesson drawn, and still promulgated, by the most prominent business gurus and consultants is that the reversal of orthodoxy is essential to future competitive success (Kanter, 1984; Peters and Waterman, 1982). Employee empowerment rather than disempowerment is the key to business advantage, requiring the rejection of adversarial tendencies and the promotion of more humane and effective alternatives to Taylorism and Fordism.

Judgements about the scale and difficulty of this project differ significantly, however. Some envisage a fundamental break with the past, a paradigm shift from authoritarianism to empowerment as competitive imperatives effectively overturn orthodox instincts and preoccupations (Womack et al 1990; Kenney and Florida, 1993; Foy 1994). The logic of survival ostensibly forces the issue for employers, requiring them to adjust to the new reality or run their businesses into the sand. Prescriptive writers and consultants often deploy this imagery to justify their own role as enablers, helping managers to make sense of the changing environment, and to renounce 'the boss' concept as they coach their employees into more conducive forms of co-operative working (Johnson and Redmond, 1998; Khan, 1997).

Though widely rehearsed, this vision imputes an unwarranted degree of rationality to employee empowerment. It becomes the inevitable and technical consequence of enlightenment, rather than a highly charged, potentially fraught and problematic process. The rhetoric of imperatives rigidifies the connection between markets and labour management, deflecting attention from intervening factors and portraying managers and workers as ciphers that passively respond to broader economic exchanges.

This was demonstrated to compelling effect on British television in 1995. Some powerful programming that initially set out to exemplify the technical and prescriptive approach and to mobilise support for empowerment, inadvertently exposed the limitations of an over-rationalised view. Enthusiast and facilitator, Sid Joynson, was followed into six organisations by a BBC camera crew that expected to capture exemplary footage of empowering practices that were not only in tune with competitive requirements but capable of inspiring practitioners in other contexts. Instead, in the first episode, they revealed the shock and disbelief of a considerate and well-meaning consultant who was forced to confront some unpalatable and unanticipated realities (O'Reilly, 1995).

After two days of working with shop floor staff at the Ipswich factory of manufacturer Videoprint, Sid listened to their presentations to the management team, fully expecting a positive reaction and a commitment to continue with empowerment in the future. This was the logical consequence of demonstrating the specific benefits that could be realised in this case, or so it was imagined. The workers, for their part, had warmed to the challenge of proposing improvements, overcoming some initial scepticism to clean the workspace, rewrite parts of the training manual to make it accessible to new recruits, and boost productivity by cutting the time taken to put inlays into video boxes. Projecting an obvious sense of achievement, Sid and the workers paused to hear the appreciative comments of managers. They were to be disappointed.

The managers took their cues from the Director, Brian Bonner, who triggered dramatic changes of mood and body language with his first response, 'I expected more'. Others then rounded on the proposals, announcing, for example, that staff already had a responsibility for cleaning and housekeeping. At this point, it became too much for the consultant to take: 'You've made me look an absolute, complete berk. They told me you would do this and I told them, "no they will not. They will come and support you", and look what you've done...Can you feel what your doing to them? Can you feel what you are doing to them?' More intense exchanges followed, peppered with personalised and abusive remarks, and prompting a walk-out by most of the workers, who then turned to the cameras to express their anger and disgust at the events inside (BBC, 1995).

This was absorbing television. It departed from expectations, and in the process exposed the shortcomings of the over-rationalised, technical-prescriptive approach to empowerment (Collins, 2000). While Sid enjoyed a significant measure of success with his employee workshops, he was ill-equipped to deal with problems that very obviously have a bearing upon attempts to change established patterns of management and organisation. His sense of the competitive advantages to be gleaned from empowerment blinded him to the potential for conflict that lies within attempts to roll out or cascade exemplary developments. In common with consultant and guru accounts generally, Sid offers a discourse on empowerment that misrepresents the dynamics of employee relations, overstating managerial responsiveness and deflecting attention from the accumulated insights and experiences of working life. With so much of the prescriptive effort devoted to presenting success stories and exemplary snapshots that showcase empowerment as a business solution (Johnson and Redmond, 1998; Peters and Waterman, 1982; Robson, 1988), the messy complexities of workplace behaviour and the problematics of retaining momentum behind practical initiatives are left unattended. Sid's application of the prescriptive approach has simply been subjected to a more immediate and dramatic examination than most.

For social scientists, the Videoprint episode is far from exceptional, the only surprise being that the resulting footage draws such an effective contrast between 'reality television' and the usual demonstration effects of business media. Scholars have argued for some time that the guru movement is theoretically and methodologically weak, and so offers an insubstantial foundation for promotional activities (Collins, 2000; Burnes, 1998). In social-scientific terms, it trades in superficial imagery, without an adequate theoretical and empirically grounded understanding of everyday life in modern organisations, which is ironic given that contributors are usually celebrated for their industry ties and management connections (see Johnson and Redmond, 1998, for example). What it offers is spuriously practical, short on substance and long on exhortation, touching commonsense notions about what management should or may involve, but without conceding the complexity of workplace relations.

As the videoprint episode demonstrates, empowerment is controversial rather than straightforward, contested and not the inevitable result of enlightenment. Regardless of the benefits that can be ascribed to it, tensions do not dissolve rapidly or automatically. Nor can they be treated as side issues that only inhibit progress in unhealthy organisations. The Videoprint experience cannot be explained away as an unusual or atypical case. Other prescriptive writers have experienced similar problems with obstructionist behaviour (Ward, 1996) and 'thinly disguised contempt' (Nicholls, 1995), sharing Sid's frustration and even his propensity to castigate those with the urge to over-control their employees. However, the most telling similarities are to be found in their conceptualisation and tendency towards a superficial appreciation of relevant issues. This is usually betrayed by the banality of the 'solution' to hostility or resistance, which typically involves positive reinforcement with staff development and the creation of a supportive climate via promotional slogans, posters and mission statements (see Chapter 4). For social scientists, adverse reactions are not so easily contained. Nor are they so readily susceptible to economic influences. In fact, they point to the significance of a remarkably stable set of attitudes and orientations that render the idea of a straightforward paradigm shift unrealistic. Some assessments are even more pessimistic, suggesting that intervening attitudes, values and beliefs effectively undermine progressive inclinations, ensuring a continuity with the past and a recasting of empowerment as neo-Taylorism, as more of a variation than a departure (Adler, 1993).

LOCATING THE POWER IN EMPOWERMENT

For prescriptive commentators such as Peters, Kanter and Sid Joynson, managerial opposition to employee empowerment is irrational and unhealthy. From their standpoint, there is nothing to fear or to reasonably argue against. Empowerment serves the economic and social self-interests of modern professional managers, enhancing their ability to mobilise resources and secure organisational objectives. By giving workers a measure of decision-making power, managers are exploiting the knowledge and capabilities of staff more effectively, improving their own results, and consequently their professional and personal standing, at the same time. This explains Kanter's view that 'delegation does not mean abdication' (1979, p. 73). Empowerment is conceptualised as a positive-sum activity that adds to the overall stock of power in a double win situation that favours workers and managers alike (Foy, 1994). Rational managers who allocate power to their subordinates will capture the attention of executives, shareholders and competitors, enlarging rather than depleting their own capacity for influence as their departments or work teams outperform those governed by more conventional, Tayloristic measures.

Despite the resources and activity levels invested in promoting this prescriptive logic, important theoretical questions remain unanswered. Is power really a resource that can be given or, for that matter, taken away? Should empowerment be regarded as something that is 'done' to marginalized workers by the more enlightened of corporate power-holders?

Curiously, this conceptualisation is endorsed and rehearsed by some of the most vehement critics of the prescriptive and managerialist approach. A significant number of social theorists accept that power is a resource in the hands of managers, and that their capacity for exerting influence is extended rather than damaged by empowering workers (Lukes, 1974). The basis for their criticism is to be found in the assessment of outcomes, as opposed to theoretical underpinnings. The positive-sum optimism of the enthusiasts is replaced with a zero-sum depiction of winners and losers, with managers expanding their power base at the expense of their employees.

From this angle, the managerial interest in empowerment has more to do with control than competitive concerns about quality, flexibility or market responsiveness. It serves an ideological purpose, concealing deep-rooted beliefs about the legitimacy of hierarchical authority, and making the extension and consolidation of managerial prerogatives seem more palatable to staff. The purpose of empowerment is not to give power to employees, but to take it away, to masquerade for greater managerial control over the nature and intensity of the work process (Yates *et al.*, 2001; Harley, 1999). In effect, the heirs to the Taylorist tradition use empowerment as doublespeak to sweeten manoeuvres that workers might otherwise resist thereby consolidating established power relations and reducing the potential for any independent challenge to managerial decisions (Lukes, 1974).

It is ironic that such polarised judgements, attributing overwhelming collective gains and debilitating sectional costs to employee empowerment, should flow from similar conceptual underpinnings. The theoretical images that tie them together are more significant than the evaluations that divide them, however. The most obvious weakness is to be found in the common assumption that the acquisition and application of power is unambiguous, uncontested and non-problematic. This crucially ignores the significance of countervailing power and the impact of contested interests and struggles that characterise relationships between people.

Judgements about empowerment that flow from the aggregate models of positive or zero-sum are unreliable because, at root, they trade on a basic misunderstanding of the nature of power. As noted, both camps present it as a resource, a quantity (Collins, 2000) or capacity (Hindess, 1982) that can be expanded or deployed at will by self-interested managers. This conceptualisation leaves no room for choice, interpretation or reaction, and assigns no weight to reflections and actions other than those of a controlling elite. This amounts to a restrictive approach, deflecting attention away from the processes of negotiation through which people exercise agency and demonstrate their own ability to act, react and interact with their working environment.

Contrary to the aggregation logic, power cannot be associated with fully predictable and inevitable results. Nor can it be reduced to a one-way process in which a unified group of managers act on 'subjects' either for good or ill. There is a strong tradition of social research that highlights the pertinence of human independence and resilience, demonstrating that people are generally very good at exerting influence over their own lives, without the mediating effect of managerial or other professional expertise (Roy 1969; Sayles 1958; Noon and Blyton, 1997). There is already some research evidence to suggest that employees actively question and often challenge management-inspired empowerment schemes, compromising declared aims and occasionally derailing them in practice. Collins (1999) and Graham (1994) provide powerful examples of shop floor action against management teams that were demonstrably, or by their own admission, changing working arrangements under the banner of empowerment. These workers retained the ability to scrutinise and influence, taking steps to empower themselves in ways that thwarted management ambitions. In the Graham case, female employees were moved to rebel against management images of empowerment that demanded flexibility, including short-notice overtime working that complicated domestic and child care arrangements without offering valued gains or compensations in return.

This highlights the importance of reciprocal interactions at the workplace and the potency of the psychological contract, the shifting sense of mutual obligations and exchanges that affects the conduct of employee relations. The message from this tradition of social science is that people have independent qualities, to a greater or lesser extent, exhibiting reflective capabilities and forms of expression, even in difficult situations (see Roy, 1973). No matter how imbalanced they may be in terms of resources, people are adept at reading and interpreting relationships through their own priorities and preferences, and of responding in a fashion that affects their experience. Hence actors in subordinate positions are never wholly subservient or compliant. Force does not of necessity bring submission. Managerial authority and rationality may fail to inspire. Employees may be impervious to incentives or moral exhortations. These insights effectively challenge the proposition that managers can exercise power, give it or take it away, in the fashion that aggregate accounts of positive or zero-sum suggest.

The realm of independent reflection and subjective action points to a more ambiguous and ambivalent set of relationships between people at work than is typically acknowledged in promotional and dismissive accounts of empowerment. The corollary is that empowerment specifically, and management decision-making more generally, cannot be seen as having a straightforward, top-down impact on outcomes. A more sophisticated conceptualisation is required to capture the complexity of reciprocal interactions, and the mediating influence of interpretations, choices, values and beliefs. A more plausible and conceptually robust view is that power is not a resource but a relational phenomenon, not a quantity or capacity but a variable quality of the interdependent relationships between people:

> Yet power is not a substance to be chopped up and weighed out in discrete lumps, like dough on a pastryboard. It is a characteristic of the relationships between individuals, groups and classes, as well as being the object of tension within and between them (Schuller, 1985, p. 32).

In truth, power has no meaning outside of the dynamic relationships between people. It is embedded in their attitudes and actions towards each other, emerging from the exchanges between them rather than distributed as a property of some rather than others. Power in this sense is interactive, relational and networked, arising from mutual interdependencies and therefore subject to ongoing struggles and negotiations. Every manifestation of power is liable to change through the ebb and flow of responses, challenges and influences as reciprocal encounters and exchanges unfold. Power relationships are all embracing but they are not overwhelming, determining or static. As people interact, they exhibit agency and experience constraint, not as equivalents but as a quality of fluid relationships that have an ever-present potential for reinterpretation and change.

Even in extreme moments or situations, when the lines of influence seem entirely clear, as between master and slave, for example, or in 'total institutions' where authority is applied in order to change the identities of inmates in prisons or mental hospitals (see Goffman, 1961), it can never be assumed that the 'poorer' relations are so completely subordinated that all scope for personal expression is removed or denied. Thinking and acting can find an outlet and muster influence to retain a sense of selfhood, from clandestine attempts to tarnish food or damage property through to overtly challenging activities such as escape or resistance. The patterns of reflecting and reciprocating may vary enormously between the disadvantaged in such situations, yet they impinge upon the interests and activities of the more prominent actors, exposing the conditionality of their position. The influence of one party can only be understood in terms of their relational interdependency with others.

Of course, human agency cannot easily be separated from the structure or contextual circumstances in which it occurs. The relationships between people are played out against a shifting backdrop of economic, technological and environmental conditions that affect cognitive and social processes. Yet these can be accommodated without accepting the fatalism of the dismissive critics of empowerment or the determinism of the promotional consultants and gurus. The apparently inexorable effects of marketplace and technology have in reality to be balanced against the self-mobilising agency and relational activities of actors, recognising both aspects, structure and agency, macro and micro, as mutual influences, each acting upon the other rather than operating according to straightforward causal principles. These interconnections between macro and micro factors produce fluctuating inequalities of power and degrees of flux and instability in the relationships between people that are mirrored in empowerment initiatives.

Historical studies of employee participation schemes have already demonstrated the significance of these inequalities and instabilities, and the struggles around them. Writing in the 1970s and 1980s, Harvie Ramsay established that periods of expanding interest and activity coincided with particular phases of the business cycle, specifically with buoyant economic conditions and tight labour markets (Ramsay, 1977, 1980). These conditions alter the terms of exchange and struggle between managers and employees, as tensions heighten and managerial authority is challenged more directly by organised labour and by the performance problems that arise from staff turnover, shortages and industrial unrest. In their efforts to contain grassroots behaviour under these circumstances, managers have turned in significant numbers to participation practices, seeing them as a means of appeasing workers and of 'regaining control by sharing it' (Fox, 1971). Increases in the incidence of participative management have not been matched historically by improvements in scope, substance and longevity, however.

The heightened interest in participation during these periods of expansion, at least until the 1980s (Ackers *et al.*, 1992), must be seen as the product of particular conditions of struggle and relational influence where managers were responding to 'pressures from below'. They were not generally demonstrating a commitment to participation *per se.* Indeed, there is evidence that management-initiated schemes were informed by a widespread antipathy to any dilution of managerial prerogatives (Ramsay, 1980, 1985). The choices and decisions that extended participation were influenced by the self-empowering activities of workers and their trade unions, reflecting the difficulty of securing consent and sustaining established prerogatives within a context and through relationships that made this inherently problematic. Since their attachment to participation was largely opportunistic, these managers had few qualms about abandoning formal arrangements when the economic conditions and, by extension, the relational terms of exchange with workers changed.

This is essentially what Ramsay discovered. His research points to a cyclical pattern of participation, extending over approximately one hundred years, with periods of advance followed by decline and decay, showing no discernible improvement in levels of joint decision-taking, or in any other substantive indicator of employee empowerment overall. On this evidence, the outcomes generated within these particular conditions of struggle and in the context of these specific inequalities of power favoured defensive managerial interests. Managers with a manipulative commitment to psychological rather than objective participation (Anthony 1977), who were concerned with appearance rather than substance, were able to contain employee action and defend their prerogatives by way of transience and triviality. By their own priorities, they successfully struggled to keep joint influence within tight boundaries, restricting it to non-controversial issues and to the petty realm of decisions about 'tea-breaks and toilets', until the pressures on them dissipated and their accommodative exercises could be happily forgotten or allowed to deteriorate (Ramsay, 1980). A substantial history of disappointing outcomes does not signal a given, predictable or bitter future, however.

The important point here is that empowerment and participation schemes emerge and exist through particular conditions of exchange and struggle between interdependent people. They are not the quasi-independent creations of an autonomous and powerful group of managers, as resource models of power suggest. Their features and effects are not directly within the hands of any particular interest group or party. The managers from history that Ramsay, Fox and others regard as opponents of meaningful empowerment were successful in pursuing their objectives not because they possessed power or were able to wield it unambiguously. The reason, in fact, is that they creatively and purposefully pursued patterns of action and interaction that secured differential gains under conditions and through exchanges that were only in part subject to their influence. The outcomes were conditional, not just on economic factors but also on the opposing practices, interpretations and responses of others, which in these cases were less perceptive, imaginative and effective.

The corollary is that empowerment must be taken seriously as a precarious project, embodying fluctuating instabilities and inequalities of power as definite practices, exchanges and struggles unfold under particular conditions. Any assessment of the potential for employee empowerment, or of claims about its transformative qualities, must be based upon a detailed examination of the interpretations, interdependencies and conditions affecting the exchanges between real people in specific situations.

Judgements need to be empirically based, allowing for contradictions and slippage from the interests of any particular group, enthusiasts or opponents, who in any case are unable to predetermine outcomes or escape from conditions of struggle.

This relational approach, together with the available historical evidence, may warrant a high degree of caution, even scepticism, about the prospects for sustaining or generalising any developments towards employee empowerment, yet it locates progress firmly within the realms of reflective practice. Advancing empowerment becomes an imaginative and purposeful matter of acting, engaging and struggling under dynamic conditions. It calls for an informed activism, and has little to do with patrician endowments or guru recipes. Nor can it be dismissed as an exercise in futility, fighting against determinate forces that will always win out in the end. In relational terms, there are no determinate forces, and it is simply meaningless to conceive of terminal points of struggle from which outcomes are assured. Although conditions change, the reciprocal interdependencies between people and the exchanges, negotiations and struggles that flow from these are part and parcel of life, and hence of any activity that involves co-operation, participation or empowerment.

Within the current economic climate, there are few signs of the distinctive factors that stimulated the peaks of interest in participation over the past century. The triggers to Ramsay's cycles of participation have been effectively removed by recessionary episodes, the weakening of organised labour and the effects of globalisation (Ackers *et al.*, 1992; Ramsay, 1993). Yet struggles around participation and empowerment are alive and kicking. They are not necessarily of the same order, or even conducted so vociferously along the same axes of interest, but they are just as significant in terms of outcomes and understanding as those elucidated by Ramsay.

Some pointers towards crucial struggles under current conditions can be found in managerial reactions to downsizing and de-layering, and attendant fears about diminishing status and job loss. Available evidence suggests that calculative interests have informed many contemporary attempts at empowerment, not so much to harness the knowledge and skills of employees as to cut the costs of management and supervision (Marchington *et al.*, 1992; Denham *et al.*, 1997). Through some telling case research, and by contrast with the conventional distinction between managers and workers, Hales (2000) reveals divisions of interest within management, and corresponding struggles, that deliver conflict rather than participative decision-making:

> ...the interpretation of empowerment which senior managers enthusiastically promote is rather different from the one which junior managers reluctantly accept...empowerment programmes are as much about the putative

reorganisation of junior managers' work as any substantive increase in worker autonomy (Hales, 2000, p. 501).

Like Ramsay, Hales detects some ideological positioning around empowerment, although his contention is that senior managers are using it not to manufacture employee consent but to justify the dilution and replacement of supervisory and junior management positions. The de-stabilising effect of the struggles between these managers becomes clear as Hales develops a relational appreciation of the way that junior managers read their situation, perceiving empowerment to be a significant threat and reciprocating out of a sense of injustice by 'engineering failure' and manoeuvring combinations of language and practice to defend their own interests.

Unfortunately, in his own analysis, Hales tends to slip away from the relational position, signposting important developments yet privileging this axis of reciprocity and struggle over others. Broader concerns and indeed actors, including employees themselves, fall out of focus as managerial protectionism and calculating self-interest come to dominate patterns of thinking and acting around empowerment. This amounts to an oversimplification that takes Hales to the point of reproducing the inadequacies of a dismissive zero-sum analysis, downgrading agency and relational dynamics through the blanket treatment of sectional interests and affiliations. On this analysis, empowerment is lost in the singular struggle between fearful, oppositional junior managers and manipulative, cost-saving executives.

Connecting empowerment to the expression of local grievances is valuable analytically and should help to lever open, rather than actually foreclose, serious analysis of relevant struggles and exchanges. While calculative attempts to defend managerial interests can now be expected to affect the conduct of employee empowerment, there is no reason to privilege them theoretically or to regard them as decisive, or even materially based. It will be clear from some of the studies cited earlier that junior managers are neither alone nor united in opposing calculative and restrictive views of empowerment. Nor do they have a monopoly on the worries and grievances that are associated with practical initiatives. It is inadequate even to consider that they operate within a fully shared frame of reference that puts personal and sectional advantage above other considerations, or rules out any serious or principled engagement with employees to pursue collaborative decision making.

Whatever the contrasts between actors, be they managers or workers, attitudes cannot be assumed nor behaviour reduced to a wholly calculative assessment of material or positional interests. Personal sense-making or 'reflection-in-action' (Schon, 1983) reaches beyond matters of material advantage or disadvantage, attaching wider issues of principle to interpretations and struggles, with individuals forming associations and active alliances that express moral and ethical judgements. This raises the prospect of multiple axes and cross-cutting issues of struggle that are beyond the scope of a rigid positional or material analysis, and which call for a more open and consistently relational view of alliances as well as fractures, commitments as well as contests, principles as much as grievances, and enablers as well as constraints on the progress of empowerment.

This book aims for a more inclusive understanding of the complex mix of interests, interpretations, and struggles that surround employee empowerment, situating them within the particular conditions of their development so that outcomes can be evaluated realistically and tactically, with an eye to future prospects and in the absence of reflex judgements, wishful thinking or unwarranted pessimism. As noted in the Foreword, the purpose of the book is to connect theory, evidence and practice, enlarging our awareness of what constitutes an adequate analysis, of what needs to be taken into account to make sense of relevant processes, and to translate this into applied knowledge that can assist or support progressive programmes. The next step is to develop the relational approach, to follow through the logic of our theoretical position and take a more detailed look at the values and practices of the agents and parties associated with empowerment, the exchanges and struggles between them and the sort of contextual conditions in which particular outcomes are produced. This takes us through some of the most telling, novel and innovative tendencies of recent times, reviewing available evidence and tracking developments, instabilities and fluctuating inequalities of power through landmark projects in teamworking, user participation in technological change, financial participation and culture management. The final section then offers a view on the overall impact and lessons to be drawn from the recurring interest in empowerment and participation schemes, thereafter broaching the questions of practice, activism and regulatory structuring set out in the Foreword.

PART ONE

Contemporary Developments

2. Practical teamworking: new lyrics for an old tune?

Teamworking initiatives have been associated with employee empowerment for a large number of years, especially in operational matters where groups of people acquire formal responsibility for specific aspects of production or the delivery of particular services. The durable appeal of the topic conceals a number of distinct themes and possibilities, however, from collective monitoring of workflow, quality, and health and safety issues to multi-skilling, work restructuring and the reversal of hierarchy. Contrasting perspectives and varieties of interest are distinguished by the broad range of labels that are commonly prefixed to the term, including self-managing, self-directing, high performance, autonomous and semi-autonomous, on-line and off-line teams.

Many of the contemporary conceptualisations of progressive or alternative teams have a lineage that dates back to the middle decades of the twentieth century. Their roots can be traced to the pioneering work of consultants associated with the Tavistock Institute of Human Relations in London (Trist and Murray, 1993) and the Quality of Working Life movement, an international network connecting innovators in the Scandinavian countries, Britain, Australia, the United States and elsewhere (Davis and Taylor, 1972; Emery and Thorsrud, 1976; Mumford and Cooper, 1979). Offended by the restrictions on work under Taylorist and Fordist regimes, this community presented a moral and social vision of autonomous groups operating with a degree of freedom from management directives, and with the discretion and variety that could deliver a meaningful, enriching and productive experience. This was ostensibly in tune with the aspirations of a better-educated workforce and an expanding population of socially responsible managers, although the campaign for autonomous teams ranged beyond humanitarianism to the challenge of making the most of available technology.

As the theoretical justification for job reform developed through socio-technical systems thinking, and with attention to influential ideas about cellular production (Mitrofanov, 1966), the focus widened from individual needs and opportunities for enrichment (Herzberg, 1968) to collective responsibility for whole sections or logically coherent portions of work. By emphasising the interdependence of social and technical dimensions of organisation, pioneers such as Trist and Bamforth (1951) and Miller and Rice (1967) connected the psychological and relational aspects of work design explicitly and purposefully to the specification and application of equipment. This extended the reach of the Quality of Working Life movement, generating a greater awareness of choices and possibilities, and a propensity to challenge established images of 'given', constraining and limiting technology (Trist and Murray, 1993). It also promoted participation and empowerment, theoretically by considering the impact of systems and machinery from the standpoint of employees at the sharp end of them, and practically by supporting a relative shift from imposed 'solutions' to collective responsibility for the management, and occasionally design, of work in particular industries and companies.

The British coal industry was at the forefront of early Tavistock initiatives on the reversal of Fordist hierarchies and divisions of labour, demonstrating the commercial viability of multi-skilled, self-selecting, organizing and regulating teams as a counterweight to production and industrial relations problems (Trist and Bamforth, 1951; Trist *et al.*, 1963). The iconic status of Volvo's team-based car manufacturing plants at Kalmar and Uddevalla in Sweden may have been even more significant, adding impetus to the debate on humanistic teamworking and providing a practical edge, as subsequent sections will reveal. Certainly, when these facilities were operating (from the 1970s and late 1980s respectively), enthusiasts had a useful means of demonstrating the practicalities of their approach. Any doubts or management scepticism about idealised or impractical humanism could be challenged with inspirational case material from the far side of the North Sea.

Yet progress towards this vision of practical teamworking has often been compromised. The reform movement has suffered serious setbacks during times of recession and corporate instability, confronting frequent back-pedalling and fluctuating patterns of managerial responsiveness. In truth, business interest has often been stimulated by narrow concerns for settled staffing and consistent job performance under buoyant labour market conditions, when problems with absenteeism, recruitment and retention captured managerial attention. Against the backdrop of unemployment, or whenever depressed economic activity relegated these issues to the margins of management decision-making, the reform movement faltered, however. Interest waned, and advocates of the humanistic approach lost ground (Kelly 1985; Littler, 1985).

Economic trends over the past two decades have produced further complications, providing scope for competing conceptualisations that dilute the reformer's message. With the product market priorities of flexible, fast and quality-assured work dominating management discourse, a more commercially minded group of commentators and consultants has taken up the case for teamworking, mixing and matching ideas and language, though with very different impulses and orientations. A more assertive approach is discernible, attempting to engineer or re-engineer teamworking on a top-down basis. This has been nurtured by a plethora of 'how-to-do-it' guide books and packaged methodologies, many of them generated through the consultancy business in the United States (Peters, 1987; see also Buchanan, 2000). References to high-performance and self-directed teamworking signal the main thrust in at least part of this literature. Yet discussion of common themes such as multi-skilling, knowledge-sharing and 'front-to-back' responsibility for core processes conceals ideological differences, even by comparison with 'social engineers' at the Tavistock Institute, who were themselves criticised for trying to shape or determine employee empowerment and experience, albeit benevolently (Loveridge, 1980).

This contrast between distinctive communities of activists, well-intentioned and commercially focused, variously aiming to drive practical teamworking from above the level of the workforce, is essential to an informed understanding of the exchanges between prescriptive and promotional commentators. Although prominent, and invariably setting the agenda for managerial explorations of the topic (in management development and MBA courses, for example), these top-down scenarios typically fail to capture the dynamics of teamworking, however.

CHALLENGING THE STATUS QUO

Employees often appear as the passive subjects of teamworking initiatives, as recipients who can be expected to welcome or benefit from the interventions of more senior others. Prescriptive accounts tend to accentuate the gains for staff, and the positive contribution of innovators who are delivering something that is innately good and constructive, boosting morale, eroding divisions and demarcations, and cultivating a sense of common purpose (Semler, 1993). An idyllic image of corporate peace and collaborative working towards unitary aims is regularly traded as the antidote to workplace tension, disaffection and the damaging conflict associated with Fordism (Womack *et al.*, 1990; Oakland, 1996).

Critical accounts by social scientists have repeatedly challenged this upbeat presentation, detecting a harder edge to managerial advocacy, and even a harshness that makes references to benevolent interventions seem perverse. An influential counter-current suggests that teamworking involves more of a calculating drive to subordinate workers and to reorganise and reassert managerial controls over them, intensifying performance more subtly and to a level unmatched by autocracy and direct supervision (Parker and Slaughter,

1988; Geary, 1993; Barker, 1993; Pollert, 1996). From here, references to devolved decision-making amount to a smokescreen for more stressful and manipulative ideological controls that reduce the likelihood of damaging conflict and resistance of the sort provoked by Fordist and other noticeably oppressive systems. With teamworking, any unpalatable or difficult experiences can be attributed to peer pressure or intra-group dynamics, allowing managers to deflect attention from 'them and us realities' and recast themselves as helpers and supporters of co-operative, committed and loyal staff.

While correcting for promotional mythology, much of this literature delivers an alternative package of overstatements and 'certainties' that polarise debate while reproducing some of the inadequacies apparent in managerial interpretations. At one level, there has been a tendency to apply overly idealistic judgements, benchmarking practical initiatives against implicit principles and success criteria that devalue modest, hesitant or potential benefits, even those that seem to find favour with participants on the ground. Idealised images of craft skills and independent working patterns lie behind some of these negative judgements, as Wright and Edwards (1998) observe. Yet craft traditions are so remote from the starting point and the local ambitions tied into practical teamworking that implicit or explicit references to them are prejudicial. It is simply unfair and unreasonable to evaluate self-management or devolved decision-making against a craft-like ability to shape work arrangements and outcomes. Indeed, the corollary of this inclination is to apply standards that can never realistically be achieved or pursued through the everyday situations that confront most modern employees, producing a reflex tendency towards negativity (Geary, 1995), and to a curious moral and analytical detachment, given the critical commitment to grassroots interests.

Contradictory tendencies are also discernible in the reification of ideological control and manipulation in much of the critical literature. The potency attributed to the ideology of teams, equating them unproblematically (and often unambiguously) with intensification and corporate conformity, contributes to the mystification of team-based management, reproducing the top-down prescriptive image of executives or senior managers as the central and most capable actors in practical situations. Ironically, employee criticism is often taken as the indicator that promotional rhetoric does not match reality, and that the game is deliberately and effectively 'rigged' by corporate bosses. Abuses have been found in the familiar tactics of containment, triviality and dumping, with additional, though very focused, operational responsibilities earmarked for group decision-making, frequently through 'off-line' deliberations so that 'on-line' working is intensified and 'stressed' within existing pay rates (Parker and Slaughter, 1988).

While employee revelations about this side of teamworking are telling and often powerful, accounts that relate them to dismissive or rejectionist positions, or reduce them to a means of unmasking managerial manipulation (Geary, 1995; Danford, 1997), are unhelpful. Sharp end views are only partially considered, and with a skewed sense of agency that presents workers as interpreters rather than actors, commentators on managerial manoeuvring whose critical pronouncements can be translated into a confident case against teamworking.

By contrast with this representation, historical and qualitative studies of established initiatives reveal that workers discern advantages as well as limitations, frequently connecting these to developmental arguments, forms of activism and effective intervention (Buchanan, 2000; Wright and Edwards, 1998). In fact, employee reports provide a sobering counterweight to the spin mentality, positive *and* negative, that informs so much of the discussion around teamworking. Participant evaluations are often more measured and cautious, entertaining the possibility of favourable outcomes rather than dismissing initiatives out of hand, yet correcting for exaggerated claims and promotional rhetoric (Foster and Hoggett, 1999).

The frustrations of the past typically inform employee judgements about continuities as well as departures, extensions and variations in their work experience, along with opportunities and potential improvements that merit open-minded, though carefully qualified, support. Case evidence points to a welcome reduction in supervisory interference, directive management and Tayloristic controls in some situations, with employees reporting a greater propensity for managers to engage with them as responsible adults, rather than treating them as 'numbers', brainless automata or immature 'school kids' (Wright and Edwards, 1998; Findlay *et al.*, 2000). There are also regular references to job enhancement, with participants expressing their appreciation for even a modicum of variety or discretionary activity, where previously they suffered the deadening experience of narrow tasks and mind-numbing repetition. Although, from a distance, the scale of the reported changes can seem quite modest – adjusting equipment in the absence of line engineers (Findlay *et al.*, *op. cit.*), calling on maintenance or support staff without supervisory approval (Wright and Edwards, *op. cit.*), switching tasks with others in the team or acting on personal initiative to help them – the impact locally is often profound, delivering meaningful and welcome gains. From the standpoint of the team member, lofty judgements about the overall sameness or debilitating tokenism of devolved decision-making and controlled teamishness can be churlish. Working life is more bearable, even for some people enjoyable, as they learn to take advantage of adjustments in their situation.

Narratives from the sharp end that give some credence to teamworking sit uncomfortably with much of the established literature because they signal an independence of view and capacity for reflection that is not widely acknowledged. They defy available over-generalisations, and at the same time present a challenge to critical and managerialist accounts of a coherent and consistent restructuring of work around teams. To hear the views of employees on an historical basis, their experiences are not driven autonomously from the top by prudent, calculating or well-intentioned executives and consultants. They are not passive spectators, hapless victims or even worthy beneficiaries of the interventions of more senior others. Employees themselves are purposeful actors, shaping, as well as sensing, significant and often worthwhile outcomes.

Buchanan (2000) provides a compelling demonstration of this in a review of the early Tavistock episodes. Castigating acolytes (specifically Mumford and Hendricks, 1996) for mythologizing the contribution of Trist, Bamforth and other consultants, he explains how the 'composite' coal-getting teams that effectively established the reputation of the Tavistock Institute actually emerged from the initiatives of miners themselves. They were not invented by Tavistock innovators, but rather acknowledged, appreciated and publicised for their significance during the course of diligent research.

As they investigated the problems associated with mechanised, longwall coal mining in 1940s Britain, Trist and his colleagues discovered that workers had devised their own response to adverse conditions that made it dangerous to operate extended seams. Celebrating developments at one mine, they detailed the advantages of the 'Manley Innovation', explaining how miners at this pit resorted to team-based coal cutting, using their own knowledge to work flexibly, allocating and rotating tasks as necessary, while developing their skills and collective expertise at the same time. Despite persistent management efforts to reduce costs by enforcing longwall methods, the Manley miners defended their team practices, eventually negotiating an agreement that formalised the composite approach of multi-skilled, self-selecting groups with collective responsibility for the full work cycle. This was a pivotal episode in the Tavistock story, although standard (including textbook) accounts give little or no credit to the intuitive and creative contributions of the Manley miners.

Fortunately, more recent studies reinforce the point of Buchanan's reinterpretation, providing confirmation that worker self-activity has an important bearing upon the nature and outcomes of practical teamworking. McKinlay and Taylor (1996) provide a powerful example from case research at an electronics plant. Workers at this site were alert to team talk and tactics, seeing through the hoopla that managers attached to their initiatives, and even turning them to some collective advantage. The most obvious indicator was that staff deliberately and skilfully undermined an individualised appraisal system, using team targets and performance figures to defend members who were singled out for management criticism.

On this evidence, work teams are not self-evidently the source of management solutions. Nor are workers easily transformed into compliant and passive team members. The nature and outcomes of practical teamworking are contested. Participants are active, and their self-activity holds out the promise of potential benefits. This is not to deny the costs and negative consequences reported by the critics, for teamworking can certainly take its toll. The point is to put negotiation, struggle and intervention at the centre of analysis, as explained in the previous chapter.

Team members are 'close to the action', and can be expected, as reflective agents, to be acutely aware of what helps and hinders, of the unfolding features of a team initiative that variously improve, complicate or damage their situation at work. To judge by available case reports (Foster and Hoggett, 1999; Wright and Edwards, 1998; Findlay *et al.*, 2000), very few participants offer unequivocal or strident judgements one way or another, negative or positive. Many are attuned to the mixed blessings of change, and are genuinely torn in their evaluations. In fact, a range of opinion is discernible, with varying emphases and contrasting judgements as people assign relative weight to more or less favourable aspects in a manner that reflects their background, outlook and orientation.

In one of the most sensitive and discriminating discussions of workforce opinion, McCabe (2000) claims space for considered views that are simply ignored in the polarised accounts of dismissive and managerialist commentators. These are apparent in shop floor reactions to teamworking at a British car company, which he elaborates under the labels 'bewitched', 'bothered' and 'bewildered'. Those in the first category accentuated the positive aspects of teamworking, mainly from an acute sense of personal disadvantage under previous arrangements. Team initiatives released them from some of the restrictions and drudgery of Taylorised jobs, so they embraced them as the basis for a more meaningful and even lucrative experience. Jonah was one of the most vocal respondents in this group, detecting an opportunity to develop and demonstrate his capabilities, to get ahead and perhaps aim for promotion: 'The frustration of a lifetime was channelled into teamworking and, therefore, it was viewed as his saviour' (McCabe, 2000, p. 210).

Others were more cautious, even negative in their assessments, qualifying Jonah's sense of improvement or criticising his gullibility. Employees who were 'bothered' by teamworking took exception to the spin in management pronouncements and official commentaries. This was a bugbear that either took the shine off worthwhile improvements or served to camouflage less palatable tendencies. The more forceful critics saw an attempt to veil stressful change with hollow posturing and patronising gestures. More tolerant opinion conceded the potential for improvements, though sought to puncture official claims. All of the respondents in this category were attuned to the stresses and strains of teamworking, and could demonstrate the impact of 'sloping shoulder syndrome' (Foster and Hoggett, 1999) as their groups assumed additional roles and responsibilities, and became more accountable for performance improvements.

McCabe's final group of respondents showed no apparent sense of novelty or impact in the transition to teamworking, and seemed to be puzzled by the fuss that it generated. By contrast with those who were 'bewitched' and 'bothered', 'bewildered' employees found little to commend or condemn it, sensing only background noise to accompany the main experiences of their working lives. There was little to suggest that they were moved or motivated, cynical or hostile. Teamworking left them cold. This is consistent with broader evidence, both on employee indifference to change programmes at work (Ogbonna and Wilkinson, 1990) and on the failure of culture-moulding interventions that target 'hearts and minds' (Ichniowski *et al.*, 1996). In fact, these studies point to additional categories of response that extend McCabe's classification, bringing in those who are offended rather than 'bothered', for example, and including those who 'go through the motions', become resigned or exhibit 'deep acting' rather than express encouragement, approval or compliance.

By acknowledging a variety of employee interpretations and reactions, the studies reported here exhibit a sensitivity and respect for otherness that contrasts markedly with the popular discourse on teamworking. They recognise that team initiatives are embedded within distinctive social, organisational and historical contexts, and so develop in a fashion that ranges beyond the scope of technical or prescriptive definitions. Individual interpretations and responses are filtered through their reflective sense of self, of earlier life experiences and future expectations, and are not therefore reducible to a uniform set of cause and effect relationships (Martin and Fryer, 1975; Storey and Sisson, 1993).

People do not react in the same way; hence teamworking is a diverse phenomenon that covers a complex mix of practices, processes, experiences, reactions and potentialities. It is charged and fraught, problematical and contested, political rather than unitary, often magnifying differences between participants and raising tensions on the shop floor. A destabilising effect is discernible, especially when opposing views trigger a clash and subsequent deterioration in sociability. This can be across managerial boundaries or among workers themselves. McCabe's case company provides an example of the latter, as Jonah's enthusiasm for teamworking prompted feelings of embarrassment in others that could spill over into resentment and bitterness, particularly when managers called him from the workspace to impress customers and outsiders.

Exchanges at this level of involvement compete with rhetorical accounts of teamworking, undermining the certainties of rigid analyses, whether positive or negative, and demonstrating the political nature of outcomes and evaluations. By calling attention to agency and negotiation, struggles and interventions, they also raise the intriguing possibility of nurturing alternative and innovative forms of practice that challenge narrow and constraining conceptualisations within organisations. In light of this evidence and by these insights, contextualising knowledge can be applied to influence the fortunes of teamworking, to identify promising and damaging circumstances and recognise patterns of progressive struggling that build resilience and enhance the collective capacity to secure benefits and limit costs.

POLITICS AND CONTRADICTIONS

Progressive images of teamworking are often presented in a very confident and assured manner, as if proponents occupy some unassailable intellectual and moral high ground. This was certainly the case through much of the 1970s and 1980s, when reformers were claiming relevance on the strength of powerful demonstration experiments, especially at Volvo where there seemed to be evidence of viable humanistic manufacturing to confound sceptical or critical opinion (Mumford, 1979; Mumford and Hendricks, 1996). In 1989, when Volvo brought its most advanced team-based facility on-line at Uddevalla in Sweden, the plant manager claimed triumphantly: 'this isn't just new production technology. It is the death of the assembly line' (Berggren, 1995, p. 278).

Uddevalla marked a watershed for enthusiasts, operationalising parallel whole-car assembly in the key strategic sector that had established linear, short-cycle task execution as the norm for productive working. This was poetic justice, a vindication for alternative thinking at the heartland of Fordism. The innovations at this site incorporated inventory and materials handling, tooling and engineering design, payment and grading arrangements, as well as the social organisation of work. Here, apparently, was an integrated facility with a consistent set of arrangements that allowed teamworking to flourish.

Material handlers worked collaboratively to organise the distribution of car kits to parallel assembly stations or 'docks' that delivered an independent full-build programme covering various model types and specifications. This meant that forty teams of approximately ten workers each dealt with between thirteen hundred and seventeen hundred components, all of them delivered in a package by computer-guided 'taxis'. Cars were built from the ground up, with completion times ranging from 1.5 to 3.5 hours. Enabling equipment was devised and installed to facilitate collaborative working, including tilting and revolving platforms to support the emerging vehicles and flexible hand tools that could be adjusted to the physical characteristics of the workers. Team members managed task allocation, quality control and testing, as well as problem-solving and dock maintenance. They even contributed to the annual round of product and process engineering, specifying suitable assembly methods and tooling adjustments to accommodate model upgrades. Pay was related to knowledge and hence group flexibility, individuals qualifying for the top rate when they could demonstrate 'whole-car competence', a grading that required sixteen months experience and the demonstrable ability to complete a test car in twenty hours with no more than four minor defects.

With such an innovative and dramatic departure from traditional forms of car-making, the confidence attached to the reform agenda during this period is perhaps understandable. However, it was severely, and all too rapidly, dented when Volvo closed Uddevalla in 1993. To many howls of disappointment and disapproval, the company dissociated itself from the 'noble experiment in humanistic manufacturing' (quoted by Berggren, 1992, p. 239), transferring production to a more conventional plant near Gothenburg. Volvo, it transpired, had more than one management regime, and as it confronted mounting difficulties through the recessionary years of the early 1990s, more traditional management ideas and values held sway. With depressed markets, plummeting sales and excess capacity testing management decision-making, conservative forces and conventional business thinking took hold, reducing Uddevalla to the status of a dispensable satellite plant, a costly blot on the accounts that could be sacrificed to restore the general health of the organisation.

Some sections of the business media immediately jumped to the conclusion that humanistic teamworking is uneconomical (Wickens, 1993). Closure was equated with failure, providing proof that work reform is 'a dead horse' (a phrase that James Womack applied to Uddevalla in a *New York Times* report on 7th July 1991). Sources of competitive advantage were now to be found in Japan rather than Sweden, specifically in the organisational apparatus of lean production with its sequential, interlocking assembly teams, intensive yet fragmented working patterns and off-line 'improvement' meetings (Womack *et al.*, 1990; Conti and Warner, 1993). This was the logical successor to the traditional assembly line, a less challenging format for those versed in Fordism and ideologically opposed to Uddevalla. From this standpoint, the distractions of work reform could finally be left behind, discarded as an outmoded deviation from superior developments in linear teamworking, or what Wickens (1993) described as controlled Taylorism.

Of course, such a sweeping dismissal triggered fierce reactions from researchers within the work humanisation community (Sandberg, 1993, 1995; Berggren, 1992, 1995), and not without justification. Tolerant opinion, expressed over the past decade and more, generally agrees that the closure decision cannot be reduced to a test of humanistic manufacturing (Adler and Cole, 1993). There was simply too much going on within the company.

Internal politicking and manoeuvring proved crucial, as stakeholders at the various plants – managers, workers and unions – struggled for position, jobs and influence. The existing structure of the company favoured the traditionalists at Gothenburg, who could link the market and manufacturing capacity issue to the unhindered and uninterrupted operation of broader engineering and product design facilities, which were also located at this traditional centre of operations. If Uddevalla was treated merely as a remote and under-utilised assembly operation, for products that were losing market share, then it could easily be considered redundant. Senior management changes made this a more likely interpretation, as, for example, the sitting chief executive who was associated with Uddevalla gave way to another with no personal ties to the plant. Again, if reduced to a capacity and convenience matter, closure could seem rational, a feeling that was likely to be magnified at the senior levels when the more powerful unions at Gothenburg mobilised to save local jobs at the expense of satellite plants (Berggren, 1992).

In reality, politics informed the closure of Uddevalla. It could not be attributed to the systematic appraisal of contrasting production methods, or to any conclusions about the relative viability of dock assembly in the developing car market. Indeed, enthusiasts have argued with conviction that Uddevalla was closed despite its commercial viability, in a display of myopic business thinking that patently ignored significant indicators of future advantage (Sandberg, 1993, 95). In one of the most rigorous and thoroughly researched ripostes, Berggren (1992, 95) contradicts the negative claims about Uddevalla, revealing crucial productivity, quality and flexibility improvements over the lifetime of the plant.

Assembly time per unit was cut by 50 per cent, giving Uddevalla an edge over Gothenburg on the work hours necessary to complete each car by November 1992, the month in which closure was announced. Berggren's figures on this are supported by earlier data from Sandberg (1993), refuting the argument by Womack, Jones and Roos that dock assembly is relatively inefficient. Uddevalla was also ahead on quality and flexibility, factors that are widely associated with competitive advantage in the car industry, though with little apparent impact on Volvo decision-making.

Within a year of operation, Uddevalla's quality rating was on a par with Gothenburg, the internal index giving it a higher points score from 1991 onwards.   Management figures show that model upgrades were accommodated more efficiently, with cost and productivity savings of between 25 per cent and 50 per cent over the more conventional facility. Uddevalla was also more effective in linking production to customer demand, altering the balance between stock and ordered cars, the latter increasing from 20 per cent to 70 per cent of total output by November 1992. The corresponding figure at Gothenburg was 35 per cent, most of the output here incurring storage and occasionally discount costs with a time lag before value was realised in the depressed markets of the early 1990s. According to Berggren's interview data, and by his collation of internal documentation, Uddevalla was acknowledged to be Volvo's internal benchmark on market responsiveness and customer satisfaction when the closure was announced. There was also a sense, expressed at least by local managers, that significant improvements and potential gains had yet to be tapped. This accounts for much of the frustration generated by the closure, and also the persistent argument that it represents an economic loss.

During the intervening years, managers in other areas have shown considerable sensitivity to the association of teamworking with quality, flexibility and market responsiveness.   Major companies have replaced assembly lines with variants of dock manufacturing at sites throughout the world, justifying the change with essentially the same points that Berggren and Sandberg registered about Uddevalla and the car market. Confronting intense competition during the late 1990s, American domestic appliance manufacturer, Maytag, reorganised factories in Iowa and Tennessee for the stationary, whole-product assembly of top-end washing machines and dishwashers. The expressed purpose was to align production with customer orders, rather than build to internal forecasts or to replenish stock. Cellular teams, as they were labelled in this case, had the flexibility to complete any model in their particular product range, at any point in their working day, improving capacity utilisation by responding directly to the orders submitted by sales departments. The Tennessee dishwasher facility was credited with improving quality by 55 per cent, cutting work in progress by 60 per cent, increasing capacity by 50 per cent and releasing 43,000 square feet of factory space (*The Economist*, 2001).

A similar reorganisation of camcorder manufacturing occurred at Sony in 2002. Reversing a strategy of low-cost mass production centred on Chinese assembly lines, the company redirected investment towards cellular working in Japan. Towards the end of the 1990s, it became clear to Sony executives that existing manufacturing strategies were dramatically out of line with patterns of demand, especially in the American marketplace where newer and more innovative camcorders quickly captured attention, and where internet sales were putting a premium on rapid delivery. Competing on price with cheaper, low-margin, yet relatively dated models was proving ineffective and costly. The move to stationary cell-based working with multi-skilled teams of employees made it easier for Sony to adjust production and respond to fluctuating demand, cutting the inventory and discounting costs associated with mass-produced models at the same time (*Financial Times*, 2003).

Sony and Maytag are among the most prominent organisations that in recent times have associated themselves with the pioneering traditions of autonomous or decentralised group working. There are many others, large and small, public and private, manufacturing companies and service providers, from the English company, Griggs, that uses 'pod production' to create Dr Marten shoes (BBC, 2002) to health care teams in the NHS (Beirne, 1999). Clearly, the demise of Uddevalla did not signal the end of parallel assembly, or demonstrate the folly of workplace restructuring as Wickens and others anticipated. However, the pre-Uddevalla preoccupation with outcomes, and the confident yet mechanical association of competitive advantage with effective, sustainable teamworking, lingers on. Much of the continuing interest is founded upon the assumption that conditioning pressures, the evident forces of consumerism, competition and devolution, are pushing unambiguously in the same direction. The clearest lesson from the Volvo experience is that this sort of economic determinism is misplaced. Conducive forces do not deliver automatic improvements at the workplace, or trigger internally consistent and coherent restructuring programmes.

By demonstrating that a good case doesn't guarantee success, the closure of Uddevalla injected a welcome measure of sobriety to the work reform movement. Patently, parallel teamworking is not all things to all people. It is difficult rather than straightforward, socially constructed rather than dictated by commercial or technological requirements. In stark contrast to initially upbeat and later romantic accounts, Berggren's post-mortem studies of the Uddevalla experience provide a 'warts and all' insight into the complexities of establishing and sustaining principled teamworking. He resists any inclination to gloss over difficult episodes or ignore setbacks and complications, thereby reaching beyond the familiar decontextualised description of the novel team structure at Uddevalla.

One of his key findings is that contradictory tendencies inhibited progress through the first two years or so, as traditional management policies, standards and administrative structures coexisted with the innovative shop floor arrangements. As a consequence of this, work teams were supplied with procedures and methods documentation that was informed by the

Gothenburg operation. Conventional management thinkers, who were housed in a detached office block away from the assembly docks, were adhering to a logic that was at odds with the team structure. Personnel at the innovative parts of the plant were actively resisting these conservative influences, often ignoring contradictory guidelines yet struggling to develop parallel assembly without conducive support systems or a consistent network of central services. Adler and Cole (1993) provide corroboration for this with evidence gathered during a visit in 1991. In fact, they condemned the management approach at that stage, describing it as abandonment rather than empowerment.

Berggren adds an extra dimension, however, charting subsequent attempts to align wider organisational structures and management processes with the assembly operation. By this means, he captures something of the dynamics of practical teamworking, conceptualising it as an uneven, contradictory and emergent phenomenon, rather than a coherent, highly integrated and decisive break with the past. He acknowledges that innovation is inherently problematical, generating tensions, contradictions and struggles to address them. This reality is confirmed by the most detailed of recent case investigations, especially in the public sector.

Using comparative data on work restructuring within the Benefits Agency (a British government welfare service), Foster and Hoggett (1999) offer a critical appreciation of inherent contradictions in the management of change that unsettled staff and destabilised teamwork initiatives. Employees at the three sites investigated for this study broadly welcomed restructuring, at least at the outset. They were critical of status divisions, demarcation lines and the continuing influence of insular civil service bureaucracy. Teamwork offered an escape from the restrictions of the past, an antidote to 'them and us' tensions that characterised their exchanges with managers and claimants alike. More critical views hardened as the new initiatives developed, however.

Employees increasingly questioned the consistency of management behaviour, notably on appraisal and reward policies that were not suitably aligned to the new collective working arrangements. As a legacy of government preoccupations with public sector productivity during the 1980s, managers were operating a very mechanical approach to staff appraisal, measuring the performance of individuals by their velocity of throughput, by the volume and rate at which they processed benefit claims. This was coupled with annual appraisal interviews that were conducted by line managers, who were required to rank each worker on a five-point scale. Despite some adjustments to accommodate multidisciplinary team activities, basically the introduction of guidelines for the collective assessment of individual contributions, workers were still being evaluated by supervisors who operated in isolation, and with little or no technical knowledge about the mix of benefits and skills involved. Some workers likened the whole appraisal and reward system to factory piece rate schemes that are out of touch with the professed interest in devolved and responsive decision-making.

On this evidence, competing management priorities were pulling staff, and indeed the Benefits Agency itself, in different directions. Attempts to secure collective working and develop shared responsibilities were undermined by inappropriate appraisal and reward programmes that drained morale. This is consistent with other evidence about the disarticulation of work reform and human resource management. Buchanan and Preston (1992) and Wright and Edwards (1998) have documented the damaging impact of inflexible pay and grading systems that cut against the grain of multi-skilled, cross-functional work arrangements on the shop floor. Conducive human resource policies and practices are not the automatic accompaniment to devolved teamworking, though in their absence support can diminish and effectiveness suffer.

Similar results have been attributed to interactional constraints within (as well as between) functional areas. Indeed, intra-functional contradictions tend to have a more immediate impact than cross-boundary effects, creating flashpoints and sparking disputes that can rapidly derail welcome initiatives. The health care sector provides an obvious example. During a study of nursing empowerment in a paediatric hospital (Beirne, 1999), it was discovered that territorialism and non-correspondence in the management of everyday pressures on labour allocation quickly disrupted a project that devolved some clinical and ward management responsibilities to teams of registered, associate and assistant nurses.

Echoing the typical business case for reform, the logic here was to increase flexibility and responsiveness, to cut patient waiting times and improve the quality of care by challenging traditional demarcation lines and altering the balance of skills between health care professionals. The role and influence of nursing staff was to be enhanced. Two wards were reorganised to allow semi-autonomous groups of nurses to cater for a dedicated portfolio of patients and their families, assessing needs at the bedside, developing detailed care plans and co-ordinating contact with doctors and other professionals. Unfortunately, in practice, there was significant slippage from these principles as nurses and line managers endeavoured, by their own priorities, to cope with the throughput of patients and 'get things done'.

The unanticipated interventions of Service Managers had the most dramatic and lasting effect. These were the managers who tailored available resources across the hospital to patient demand, and the majority were interpreting their role in a fashion that brought them directly into conflict with the nurses. Responding to staffing shortages on a daily basis, what they regarded as a more pressing need than team-based care, these managers would pluck nurses out of their wards to cover work in other parts of the surgical directorate. They were also moving patients, boarding them out to make space for new admissions and to contain costs through weekend ward closure. This often occurred at night while the patients were sleeping. Children would waken in another ward, removed from their designated nursing team. The continuity of care was disrupted as nurses lost their patients, and with them the opportunity to apply the core principles behind the new initiative. Staff reactions were marked by frustration, disappointment and eventually cynicism as the logic of a specified caseload was replaced by a 'care as best you can' approach. Front-line workers in this case, as in the Benefits Agency, lost faith in the reform agenda as one set of management priorities undermined the realisation of another.

These studies have an authenticity and realism that cannot be found in static descriptions or typologies of teamwork, or in ideological treatments, be they of left or right, prescription or denial, glorification, mystification or rejection. They offer an insight into the dynamics of work reorganisation, contextualising the connections between structure and agency while magnifying processes that impinge upon the deployment and development of teamwork initiatives. They alert us to variable and evolving interpretations and provide a means of understanding the tensions that often surround practical episodes. The corollary is that teamwork survives as a potentially progressive phenomenon. It is not something that is unduly restrictive or stifling *per se*. However, its practical application often embodies inconsistencies, confusions and contradictions, which is why arrangements frequently sour as projects unfold.

For Berggren, this realisation permits learning and innovation. It highlights the importance of recognising and tackling constraints, of adjusting the focus of reform from initially specifying to actively sustaining work humanisation. His own interpretation of the Uddevalla experience culminates in a discussion of managerial adjustments and alterations through 1992. It is ostensibly from this period, the final six months or so of parallel assembly, that the most significant lessons are to be drawn.

By the summer of 1992, senior managers had acknowledged the need for consistent support systems and were introducing organisational arrangements that apparently suited the production concept. These were designed to be the logical extension of dock assembly, projecting outwards from the team structure in a way that challenged established ways of doing things while at the same time anticipating a more sensitive and 'reflective' approach to innovation. Radical decentralisation was a key part of this, reducing the hierarchy to just two tiers, plant and shop (assembly and materials handling) managers, with the latter installed in Uddevalla's principal governing committee in order to emphasise the centrality of team production. A novel leadership development programme was also launched, incorporating a requirement for managerial, professional and technical staff to serve some manufacturing time with the assembly teams. This was considered to be a useful way of fostering understanding and co-operation, qualities that were to be enhanced by relocating all managers and senior administrators to space alongside the assembly docks. Innovative measures were also initiated to ensure that product development became a more interactive process. In fact, participative working between industrial engineers and workers had reached the point where they were jointly setting requirements for designers in light of tooling and other technical capabilities, and then rearranging the workspace and available equipment to manufacture cars with the latest specifications.

By reporting these developments and exploring the problematics of alignment at Uddevalla, Berggren provides a valuable corrective to the early optimism and much of the naivety associated with the work reform movement. Having said that, it is important not to overstate managerial achievements or romanticise the shift to 'reflective production' within Volvo (or any other organisation). The fact of closure demonstrates the precariousness of practical teamworking, regardless of the steps taken to manage interactional effects, which were certainly sophisticated when judged against developments at the Benefits Agency, for example.

3.   Technology and user empowerment

The search for alternative and progressive forms of organisation has been heavily influenced by reflections upon the nature and role of work technology. Since the Tavistock mining studies (Trist and Bamforth, 1951; Trist *et al.*, 1963), researchers have been acutely aware that there are choices to be made about the organisation of human activity around a given technology. Rejecting the fatalistic argument that technology strictly determines the conduct and experience of work, enthusiasts have claimed space for humanisation, even around Fordist technologies, as the previous chapter indicated. By the late 1970s, however, this sense of choice and capacity for influence had developed to include the design and shaping of the technology itself, as opposed to job (re)design after the fact of its creation.

Socio-technical systems theorists were again at the forefront of research and activism. Indeed, it is possible to discern a second wave of interest in the principles of socio-technical design as debates around the development and deployment of computer and communications technology progressed through the 1980s (Beirne and Ramsay, 1988). With the growing realisation that organisations faced problems in harnessing the most sophisticated technology, critical accounts of rationalistic tendencies and influences on the workplace resurfaced (Mowshowitz, 1980; Briefs *et al.*, 1983). Perceptive authors realised that organisational problems were constraining technological innovation, and that this offered new opportunities, access to a new area, and a means of taking the reform message to an important category of professional actors, technologists and computing scientists (Mumford, 1983).

Following the established traditions of the reform movement, critical scrutiny provided the initial leverage to promote change. The target this time was applied science and the orthodox principles of computing design, rather than the authoritarian preoccupations of managers or legacy of Taylorism on the shop floor. By conventional accounts, the process of creating computer-based work technology proceeds through a series of detached and socially neutral techniques that deliver clarity, precision and a technically proficient operating system. The official history of the discipline is that progress has been achieved through the application of engineering principles and standards that have institutionalised control in a complex, demanding and labour-intensive activity that was previously vulnerable to errors and shortfalls in productivity and performance relative to expectations. Consequently, the common conceptualisation is of a self-contained, monolithically expert and rational discipline that thrives independently of the organisational context in which the technology is eventually used.

The management of computing development itself is typically informed by two closely connected manifestations of engineering rationality that perpetuate this image of technically dominated or technocentric design: an adherence to formal methodologies based on mathematical and logical processing techniques, and a step-wise progression through the precisely defined stages of a project life cycle. Although various brands of methodology now vie for attention, the vast majority share common characteristics and a familial tendency to lay down very precise protocols, tools and procedures for structuring the development process. The central organising vision is of a linear track through isolated compartments of work, allied to a sequential delineation of the activities that designers are expected to follow. Occasionally, the image presented is of a cascading waterfall of discrete project segments that proceed through some variant of requirements specification, outline and then detailed design, testing and implementation, with fine-tuning, maintenance and documentation incorporated at the end (Beirne *et al.*, 1998b).

For social science commentators, the similarities with Taylorism are compelling (Mumford, 1983). Common roots and characteristics are discernible in the drive to divide, standardise and formally specify the boundary lines between associated work tasks. This, in turn, reveals a corresponding commitment to top-down co-ordination and control, and to the concentration of decision-making authority among 'objective' experts, social actors who supposedly have an advantage over other stakeholders by virtue of their independent ability to create ordered systems and deliver rational outcomes. This most revealing of genealogical preoccupations translates into the systematic marginalisation of alternative interests and sources of expertise, notably workers under Taylorism and the users of technology under computing orthodoxy (Greenbaum and Kyng, 1991; Beirne *et al.*, 1998b).

Yet the parallels with Taylorism continue to hold through the reactions and controversies that have been triggered by rationalistic computing development. Since the 1980s, the pages of computing and systems management journals have been peppered with articles lamenting the limited returns on investment, persistent problems with 'usability' and high levels of frustration associated with technologies that have been created by conventional methods. There are numerous illustrations of technically interesting and sophisticated systems that failed to match their operating specifications, falling dramatically short of what people in the receiving organisations envisaged, wanted or expected. Some have been spectacular, such as those widely reported in Britain at the Stock Exchange, customs and ambulance services and at the Performing Rights Society (BBC, 1994; Flowers, 1996). There is also an abundance of anecdotal evidence from workers and mangers who bemoan the fact that remote and over-rationalised creations have little or no correspondence with the realities of their situation, and require costly amendments and organisational adaptations to secure even basic levels of performance. From this grassroots position, rationalistic computing seems vulnerable to the same basic criticism that was, and still is, levelled at the Taylorist management of labour, namely, that it's more trouble than it's worth (Mumford, 1983; Greenbaum and Kyng, 1991).

For traditionalists, of course, rationalism can be defended if disappointing outcomes are attributable to departures or deviations from the prescribed approach. Some custodians of 'good practice' have argued that systematic methods are not adequately followed by computing practitioners, that developers are not demonstrating the take-up of a 'mature' approach, and that rationalism should now be aligned with national and transnational quality assurance regimes to encourage compliance (Wilson *et al.*, 1996). This view is canvassed against a strong and rising current of alternative opinion, however. Instead of criticising developers for pursuing a lax or less than systemic approach, influential commentators are actively challenging received wisdom and registering doubts about the adequacy of the computing orthodoxy itself (Curtis *et al.*, 1988; Bansler and Bodker, 1993; Greenbaum and Kyng, 1991).

The central argument here is that the established ideal of highly structured, top-down development is just too simplistic and remote from the everyday pressures of organisational innovation, relying on abstract and over-rationalised images that are at odds with realities on the ground. The immediate context of 'live' computing projects, and the target environments for their applications, display a level of complexity and subtlety that is beyond rationalistic models. The reason, ultimately, is that they lack an informed understanding of important socio-economic factors that affect how the process unfolds. These are beyond the reach of formal modelling and data-capturing tools that privilege the more accessible, obvious and official aspects of management and organisational behaviour. As the post-mortem analyses of systems failures reveal, informal exchanges and activities that rely on tacit skills and abilities, especially under exceptional as opposed to routine circumstances, remain out of focus. Moreover, the consensus of critical opinion is that this is unlikely to change so long as the perceptions of workers and other organisational members connect the mechanical application of standard tools with the cult of the expert and the imposition of 'designer' computing 'solutions', regardless of local views and concerns (Mumford, 1983).

The corollary is that increasingly strident or strictly enforced rationalism will obstruct rather than promote the more effective application of work technology. The problems of failure and frustration will be exacerbated as the constraining influence of technocentric design fosters distrust and resistance, manifest in a reluctance to provide reliable information, a refusal to adapt to new systems, and possibly even attempts to sabotage attendant processes or outcomes. The message that comes across here is that the successful development of work technology is contingent not only upon the technical science of computing, but also a grounded understanding of human orientations and behaviour within and between organisations.

This is not in itself a novel argument, but rather a variation on long-standing themes in the computing literature. The charge that rationalists are out of touch and that their methodologies are ill-conceived has been rehearsed over four decades. During the 1960s and 1970s, penetrating critiques by authors such as Boguslaw (1965) and Weizenbaum (1976) stimulated debates about the poverty of abstract systems thinking that relegates sections of humanity to the status of machine substitutes, that promotes a concern for 'non-people' rather than developing human roles and relationships through technological innovation. From here, technologists have no effective means of engaging with people who have relevant work or business knowledge because they reject their input ideologically, and exclude them by design. The corresponding call for root and branch change, for a more open and inclusive approach that anchors technology to the interests and knowledge of those on the receiving end, left many practitioners unmoved until recently, until the facts of failure and frustration became so glaringly obvious. Now there are signs that client communities and user groups have sufficient confidence to express their concerns about emerging technologies, and to challenge the internal logic of engineering rationality. User groups are certainly more vocal about the limitations of computing orthodoxy and the litany of empty promises associated with its application (Beirne *et al.*, 1998a; Greenbaum and Kyng, 1991). There is also evidence that user managers are acting purposefully to influence the economics of systems development, rather than passively accepting rationalistic prescriptions and the attendant costs of adhering to more rigidly defined methodologies (Beirne *et al.*, 1998b; Bansler and Bodker, 1993; Guidon and Curtis, 1988).

Commercial systems builders are confronting this in the marketplace, reporting that clients are pressing them to contain costs and provide a responsive service, requirements that sit uneasily with rationalistic drives to benchmark their performance against tighter engineering standards and process controls. Responding to the commercial context in which they operate, some front line developers, notably those working for small to medium-sized systems providers, are negotiating their way around formal methods that are felt to be hampering their efforts. Their clients are effectively forcing their hand, asserting managerial influence and restricting the levels of delegated control available to computing 'experts' (Beirne *et al.*, 1998b). Bad experiences and the reported failures of the past are conditioning the contractual and everyday exchanges between users and technologists, with those on the receiving end squeezing costs and completion dates while demanding systems that are functional on their own terms, that add value to their business or operation rather than by reference to some technical and externally generated success criteria.

For developers working against these pressures, the economics of innovation put a premium on applied knowledge, on their ability to relate technical skills to an understanding of the receiving organisations and how they, in fact, can make the most of available technology. Cultivating local knowledge and the status of a trusted partner is the key to repeat business and a solid reputation for these technologists. Knowing their clients and relating technology visibly and directly to their business contexts is more important than adhering to an engineering rulebook that sets predefined procedures in stone and monitors compliance according to engineering rather than business priorities (Beirne *et al.*, 1998b). Departures from rationalism and the traditional life cycle become sensible instead of dangerous, entrepreneurial more than deviant, promoting success by tailoring the process to client concerns and avoiding the imposition of costly controls that are viewed with suspicion (on documenting progress or altering specifications beyond the initial steps, for example). By this evidence and these interpretations (Beirne *et al.*, 1998b; Bansler and Bodker, 1993; Guidon and Curtis, 1988; Harding and Gilbert, 1993), engineering and organisational responses to the technology problem are far from congruent. On a broadening front, and certainly at the level of practice, the wisdom of the traditional experts, the custodians of rationalism, is questioned rather than taken for granted.

These points about the human and commercial blind spots in orthodox thinking puncture the illusion of rational design, viz., that effective technology is created by objective outsiders who are untainted by workplace preoccupations and local interests, and who promote ordered progress by virtue of their technical expertise. Patently, work technology does not develop in isolation from human and commercial considerations. Nor for that matter does rationalism since it incorporates a particular ideological treatment of people and organisation, as previously mentioned. The application of computing to the workplace has been flawed, compromised and expensive, calling doubt upon even the most ardent defence of rationalism. This reality, or rather the widespread acceptance of it, provides a powerful impetus for change.

A growing body of researchers and practitioners now accept that systems development is an integrative activity that depends entirely on the synthesis of particular socio-economic and technical processes and relationships (Beirne *et al.*, 1998b; Howcroft and Wilson, 2003). Openness and co-operation have emerged as developmental themes, as essential attributes for understanding and developing this rich mix of ingredients to the point where technology actually (rather than hypothetically) adds value to work or to business. More inclusive forms of knowledge-sharing and joint decision-making are advocated to straddle the gap between technologists and user communities in terms of their respective skills, insights and experience. User involvement and participative systems design, topics that have figured prominently in the research literature since the 1970s, are attracting greater attention (Howcroft and Wilson, 2003). The net result is that theorists and practitioners from a range of different backgrounds, and with computing, management and social science affiliations, are actively conceptualising systems development in more novel and innovative ways than hitherto. This does not signal an emerging consensus, however.

The contention that systems development should be less exclusive, more open and heavily reliant upon local knowledge is rehearsed by theorists and practitioners with very different ideas and prescriptions (Beirne and Ramsay, 1988, 1992). Some articulate a view that is striking for its continuity with the orthodoxy rather than any departure from it. Users are to be courted through amendments to rationalistic practice that focus narrowly on the challenge of extracting relevant information and generating consent for designer systems when they arrive in the workplace. This is discernible in discussions of knowledge elicitation, prototyping and overcoming resistance in the more recent packaged outlines of structured practices and formal methodologies (Blum, 1996; Yeates *et al.*, 1994). Established prerogatives and procedures are not considered to be problematical *per se*, requiring only the passive involvement of users where professional technologists deem it necessary to combat systems 'noise' or to attend to 'human factors', phraseology that usefully signals the continuing influence and limited intent of traditional thinking.

This response either rejects or fails to grasp the full significance of critical commentary, attaching a minimal, instrumental value to user input. Proponents are preoccupied with the legitimacy of design decisions and the success of their applications, rather than the advantages or disadvantages for users. The validity of such involvement is judged according to the development conditions prevailing for particular projects. Hence the importance ascribed to user roles varies with the type of system being introduced. Where effective installation is considered to be dependent on the voluntary use of the technology, as in the application of management decision support systems, for instance, involvement is put at a premium. Conversely, if design teams can be shown to contain all the expertise required, if specifications can be clearly defined, or if the product is likely to be invisible or unimportant to users, then involvement is considered unnecessary.

This is a calculative approach that maintains the divisions and top-down feel of orthodox engineering. Adherents assume, on rationalistic grounds, that computing professionals have a legitimate role to manage and control the contributions of users. While conceding that user input is potentially significant and that design is not exclusively a technical exercise, the inference is that effectiveness will be compromised if existing conventions and demarcations are challenged rather than amended. Again the implication is that users lack the necessary expertise to make an independent contribution. Indeed, they appear in these representations, not as purposeful human beings with interests and preferences, but as resources or components that can be used advantageously to improve design decisions and widen the range of options open to technologists.

Following this line, a substantial body of research has focused on the classification of conditional variables that influence the success of involvement episodes. This suggests that the impact of involvement on resistance and utilisation, and in generating information, varies with the types of user involved, the phases of development during which it is practised, and the nature of the communication processes that are brought into play. Correspondingly, guidelines on good practice have emerged that encourage designers to assess the status of users according to their knowledge or influence, and to vet candidates for involvement on whether they are likely to divulge information or promote the acceptance and effective use of systems when installed. Restricting the scope of involvement to particular stages of the traditional life cycle is also considered to be prudent. Recommendations typically centre on requirements analysis and implementation, where additional 'tools' are needed to capture data or overcome resistance to change (Wong and Tate, 1994).

By these methods, user involvement is reduced to an early warning mechanism that can let designers test out their assumptions about work situations, and head off any difficulties prior to costly disruptions. Users are conceptualised merely as intervening factors that can be dispossessed of their intrinsic knowledge and encouraged to conform to the technology process by the application of formal techniques and 'logic'. Interestingly, the question of whether users will accept involvement on these terms, or even use the process to pursue other objectives, is rarely asked. Involvement is assumed to be a concession that users cannot refuse, or a mechanism that can operate effectively where user managers demand compliance.

TOWARDS A RADICAL AGENDA

The cold calculation that informs this variant of rationalism is anathema to writers and activists versed in the participative traditions of workplace reform. From their standpoint, the advance of work technology is a social and ethical project, and not just a technical exercise. Analyses in this vein support social as well as performance goals, presenting the case for involvement not only on pragmatic grounds as an indispensable functional requirement for sound design, but also as a fair and morally justifiable course of action. Principles are at stake for this community, and the key one is that technology should be developed and modified to satisfy user interests and requirements, not the other way around.

Attempts to operationalise this alternative vision have been heavily influenced by socio-technical design ideals. Enid Mumford is the most celebrated pioneer of what is now called socio-technical systems development, an approach that presents involvement not as a communication exercise but as a legitimate right and end in itself (Mumford, 1983, 1996). Mumford and her colleagues aim to increase the potential for self-determination, rather than capture data or minimise possible resistance (Hirschheim and Klein, 1994). Drawing upon earlier generations of job-centred socio-technical theory, they blend ethical and effectiveness arguments to challenge instrumental thinking and encourage user communities to take control of the technology process.

From here passive involvement is unacceptably manipulative, and so transparent that users are unlikely to volunteer their insights, expertise and commitment on a sustained basis. What is missing is the recognition that design relates not to technical systems that have behavioural consequences, but to extensive social systems that have a technical dimension. The process of remedial activity is therefore much larger and more complex than is commonly envisaged by those who argue for restricted and constrained user involvement. Designers have to locate the technical features of new systems within a surrounding organisational framework of priorities, roles and relationships that cannot be fully appreciated by the application of passive procedures through the early stages of development when users may be unsure about their requirements and the possibilities for satisfying them. Designers must also incorporate socio-psychological phenomena if resistance is to be reduced, giving user views on work experience and job satisfaction equal credence alongside technical issues and constraints. By contrast with calculating involvement, socio-technical approaches call for a dual 'fit' between users and their 'needs' on one hand and technologies and organisational structures on the other.

The corollary is that involvement *per se* is not enough. Users must have an active role, with genuine decision-making influence. Mumford's ETHICS methodology, an acronym for Effective Technical and Human Implementation of Computer Systems, is the most widely publicised and applied means of pursuing this. As an alternative to prescriptive orthodoxy (Hirschheim and Klein, 1994), it offers what purports to be a toolkit for enacting consensus forms of user-driven, even democratic, design. Hierarchy is de-emphasised as larger numbers of stakeholders are brought into the process and given formal opportunities to influence outcomes in a concrete way. A novel mix of analytical tools is available as part of the package to elicit user views and promote a shared understanding of issues and options, including a diagramming technique to focus discussion on workflow and layout, and diagnostic questionnaires to relate personal needs and expectations to organisational priorities and technical possibilities. These provide the means of situating Quality of Working Life concerns for interesting and rewarding work at the centre of computing projects, and for retaining an everyday focus on the joint optimisation of technical resources and human effort.

Various options for structuring participation are also identified, signalling a pragmatic concern to make progress even under difficult situations that require compromise. Mumford herself proposes three categories of participation, ranging from least to most desirable (Mumford, 1980, 1981). At the conservative end of her spectrum is Consultative Design, which locates decision-making predominantly with the traditional sources of technical expertise. Users are entitled to give 'evidence' through formal procedures like interviews or questionnaires, by offering information directly, and by subjecting the final pool of knowledge to cross-examination. Representative Design gives user communities a more positive or forceful role through a formal structural mechanism such as a steering committee, or by a process of secondment where certain users sit on design teams. Representatives are chosen by various means, including appointment by managers (Mumford and Henshall, 1979) or by a ballot of users for candidates nominated either by managers or the users themselves. The formal influence of these representatives can vary from simply providing input and reporting progress to channelling user decisions on whether design options should be modified or vetoed.

Consensus Design is the most ambitions format identified by Mumford, and the one that she personally favours for its democratic characteristics. This attempts to give entire user communities the opportunity to influence decisions directly and throughout the development process. The machinery is still representative, which can be a source of confusion, though at this level there are two groups, again a steering committee and a design team, the latter including elected members and operating with a brief to develop viable options and final arrangements. The steering group consists of user managers and representatives of trade unions and other interests (such as nursing or medical personnel), and carries responsibility for setting basic objectives and constraints, for monitoring progress and ensuring that decisions are consistent with broader policies and strategic priorities.

Through three decades of practice across a range of settings, and in major organisations such as Rolls Royce, KLM and Dutch Telecom, Tetley Walker, DEC and ICI, this socio-technical approach has captured interest and approval. Enthusiasts have commended its 'emancipatory' intent and ability to deliver 'authentic' participation (Hirschheim and Klein, 1994). Others remain cautious, even sceptical, however. Hasty and unrestrained judgements can have an unsettling rather than a reassuring effect, suggesting that proponents are out of touch, or insensitive to everyday challenges and constraints. While the discussion around ETHICS and socio-technical design has played an important role in claiming space for user participation (rather than merely involvement), it may have exercised researchers more than practitioners, with little overall effect on the conduct of systems development (Howcroft and Wilson, 2003). Moreover, it trades so heavily on positive imagery and convivial possibilities that the challenges of enacting and sustaining direct participation in the technology processes are given insufficient attention.

Writers allied to the Scandinavian traditions of workplace reform have reached beyond a wider sense of unease to register some of the most telling concerns about the socio-technical approach (Ehn, 1988; Bjerknes *et al.*, 1987). Central to this is the charge that it lacks a critical edge, theoretically and practically, that it represents a conservative influence and is therefore ill-equipped to deliver authentic participation. It is considered to be tame, to pursue harmony and consensus with little obvious grasp of real world tensions and conflicting interests, making it a soft target for cynical managers or other professionals who would co-opt, manipulate or abuse the process (Bjerknes *et al.*, 1987). The potential for drift and for the watering down of any progressive intent is highlighted, along with the danger of slippage downwards through Mumford's hierarchy of participation to the point where front line users detect little more than constrained or curtailed involvement.

These critics articulate the case for a more politicised, less vulnerable and resilient approach to participative design. Although various shades of opinion inform Scandinavian commentary, and there is no single, precisely defined approach, adherents share a common antipathy for managerialism and the corporate shaping of technology. They act as advocates for user rights and align themselves explicitly with trade unions, third party organisations that carry favour for their independent ability to safeguard user interests, on the technology front as elsewhere. Consequently, their underlying conceptualisation connects technology to thorny issues of workplace control and the defence of established prerogatives that socio-technical accounts tend to miss or avoid. Their references to democracy and emancipation are therefore sharper, considered rather than bland, and developed with a greater apparent feel for the problematics of advancing participative design.

The socio-technical emphasis on consensus, harmony and mutually beneficial innovation is thrown into relief by the attention given to politics, conflict and tensions, and their resonance with the felt realities of participation on the ground, as often expressed by practitioners and users themselves (Beirne *et al.*, 1998a; Clement, 1994). The commentaries offered by Mumford and her colleagues seem aloof and sanitised by comparison, lacking the analytical wherewithal to accommodate relevant issues or counteract inhibiting tendencies. Despite their common professed commitment to democratising the technology process and humanising work, these traditions are at odds with each other theoretically and practically, with one denying that the other is fit for purpose. While they share a basic distaste for mechanical and restricted user involvement, the Scandinavian researchers fear that socio-technical approaches degenerate to this in applied content. Hence, they present a very different framework and vocabulary of practice.

To differentiate their own work from socio-technical interventions, Ehn and Kyng developed the Collective Resource Approach (Ehn, 1988; Bjerknes *et al.*, 1987). This, again, is an indicative blend of ideas and innovations from across the Scandinavian research community, rather than a unifying approach. It speaks to the wider interest in mobilising trade unions in the technology process, drawing on a productive history of cross-boundary collaboration between researchers and union activists in Sweden, Demark and Norway. This famously dates back to the mid-1970s and the DEMOS project, Democratic Planning and Control in Working Life: on Computers, Industrial Democracy and Trade Unions. 'Investigation groups' were established at a number of sites to bring workers and their unions together with a multidisciplinary research team to consider local problems and open horizons for developing technology and enhancing work experience. This was an initial, albeit rather tentative, move against the conventional logic of integrating users into the established patterns and priorities of systems analysis and implementation, exploring the potential for people to shape the nature of the technology they eventually use. Given its localised operation, it was felt to be largely reactive, an aspect that subsequent projects would tackle through a more explicit emphasis on specifying and creating skill-enhancing and socially useful technologies.

Probably the most influential and frequently cited initiative in this regard was labelled UTOPIA, Training, Technology and Products from the Quality of Work Perspective. This was initiated at the beginning of the 1980s, and set out to deliver new and highly marketable computing tools for text and image processing to the graphics industry. The challenge for the collaborators was to find ways of harnessing technology that could develop the skills and experiential contribution of employees while improving the typographical quality of newspapers. Shop stewards and members of the Nordic Graphic Workers Union participated in a design group with computing scientists and practitioners from an independent systems supplier. This was to be an arena for mutual learning and collaborative influence, with contributors applying their professional expertise and political interests to produce novel and viable technology for the marketplace, for general rather than their own immediate use.

The results attracted international attention, and are widely acknowledged to be significant. Advances are recognised in terms of the accessibility and humanising qualities of the resulting technology, and also in the pioneering methods devised for its creation (Bjerknes *et al.*, 1987; Greenbaum and Kyng, 1991). The boundaries of systems development were extended by contributions that encouraged mutual learning. Organisational simulations, distinctive prototypes and design mock-ups, even cardboard computers, enabled technologists to learn from the experiences of designated users, rather than formal systems descriptions. They were working not from abstractions but the situated actions of the people doing the work. Their interventions therefore had an authenticity that continues to draw respect in the literature (Blomberg *et al.*, 1996; Howcroft and Wilson, 2003).

Of course, there were setbacks and difficulties that also figure in measured evaluations. The participating vendor eventually stopped producing the resulting system. Trade union politics magnified the tensions that can be generated by different levels of interest, commitment and activism, even within organisations that profess to be working towards common objectives through a shared ideology. Ehn (1988) candidly admits to the fragility of these episodes, a feature that others have identified when considering how they might translate to less supportive environments, to those without the conducive legal and historical labour relations traditions that characterise the Scandinavian countries.

What they contribute, nonetheless, is a rich basis for reflection and some novel ideas about the conduct of participative design. They help to flesh out Berggren's notion of reflective production, relating issues about the consistency of progressive practice to personal sense-making about values, reactions and patterns of engagement. Reflective technologists in other countries have responded to the principles of learning and designing 'by doing', by rooting analysis in local activities and understandings and creating space for user influence through 'situated design'. A particularly influential group has emerged in the United States, preferring to talk about participatory or co-operative design, though bringing the Scandinavian work to a wider audience and sustaining the momentum behind more ambitious or radical formats (Blomberg *et al.*, 1996). This interest in the Scandinavian contributions has even prompted a revision of ETHICS and the socio-technical approach.

Responding to the criticisms levelled at ETHICS, Hirschheim and Klein (1994) have endeavoured to reformulate and reinvigorate it, to enhance its emancipatory potential. They acknowledge that the collective resource approach has made substantial progress in grounding development activities and promoting self-awareness through critical reflection about the context in which technology is actually used. ETHICS, they concede, is weak in this regard, although it could, in their view, be modified to develop these qualities in practitioners. Diary-keeping and electronic meeting systems are introduced as viable means of capturing and advertising ideas, recognising views and conducting arguments, and generally building confidence and the capacity to engage with others. However, at the core of their contribution is the contention that ETHICS has distinctive qualities in itself that make it the most viable candidate for upgrading to achieve emancipatory goals.

Ostensibly, ETHICS has an advantage as a framework that can actively support self-determination and reduce the risks of passive or manipulative user participation. While the Scandinavian interventions operate on a 'top-down' or 'outside-in' basis, the 'overwhelming emphasis on bottom-up (grassroots) participation' (p. 87) gives ETHICS an edge. This is a controversial argument that is far from secure in its attempt to answer the critics. It rests on the proposition that ETHICS has an essential integrity to its process, that it incorporates checks and balances, for example, that target negative influences and provide a compelling reason for stakeholders to collaborate in genuine and meaningful ways. Hirschheim and Klein attempt to extend and strengthen these elements to institutionalise critical reflection, mutual learning and collective influence via ETHICS. They add teamwork incentives, group decision support concepts and many of the ingredients of the collective resource approach to solidify the ETHICS methodology and secure its credentials as the most robust structure for organising participation.

Strong claims are made to support this project, although in truth the authors deliver an affirmation of faith, asserting rather than demonstrating the suitability of the host methodology. For all the emphasis on critical reflection and local influence, ETHICS is endorsed by means of abstract arguments that reflect prevailing debates within the research community, again suggesting an insularity of outlook rather than a serious attempt to act on practitioner views. Hirschheim and Klein commend their work in terms of its responsiveness to critical opinion: '...the reformulation can be called critical insofar as the underlying philosophical principles have passed the critical scrutiny of the relevant informed community' (p. 99). Grassroots practitioners with experience on the receiving end of ETHICS interventions seem to be excluded from this community. Opinion from the sharp end is conspicuous by its absence, yet the folly of endorsing the framework without such a critical reference point is apparent from available studies of ETHICS in action.

Of the various episodes reported to vindicate this approach (Mumford, 1996; Mumford and MacDonald, 1989), one stands out in terms of the frequency and positive nature of its citation (Mumford, 1980, 1981, 1996; Mumford and Henshall, 1979, Land and Hirschheim, 1983). The host company was Rolls Royce. During the 1970s, Enid Mumford was invited to operationalise ETHICS at its Derby engine plant for the introduction of a supplier's accounts system. This involved some sixty employees at the Purchase Invoice and Treasurers Departments, areas that were plagued by inefficiencies manifest in rapid staff turnover and significant delays in the payment of outstanding accounts. A design group of six clerical workers from the affected departments and two systems analysts from the management services division was established and charged with assessing efficiency and job satisfaction requirements, and for incorporating these in proposals for computer-based reorganisation. At a higher level, a steering committee of middle and senior managers, plus a trade union official, operated to review progress and arbitrate on whether design decisions complied with company policy. After some seven months of working half a day per week, the design group produced three successive designs, submitting each in turn to the management group and to employees until a version was finally settled upon and implemented.

At face value, this is an encouraging example of what ETHICS can deliver. Indeed, Mumford repeatedly presents it as an unambiguous and fairly straightforward success story. The main text says as much in a bold and unqualified opening statement (Mumford and Henshall, 1979). Land and Hirschheim (1983) describe it as a good example of the '...rare democratic for of decision making... [where] ...all participants have an equal voice in the decision process' (p. 103). Closer inspection provides good reason to doubt this, however. Problems are discernible, both in the detail of the case and the manner of its reporting. Surprisingly, significant issues and constraints on the process are glossed over, revealing a lack of critical self-reflection. More importantly, there is little in Hirschheim and Klein's reformulation to signal that they are any more sensitive or better equipped to grant them serious attention.

Firstly, the design objectives and outcomes seem to have been clearly pre-defined by senior figures. The 'Internal Consultant' on the project (and co-author of the main text) was the Systems Manager of the accounts section.

Members of the design group, supposedly the hub of the process, were hand-picked by this individual in collaboration with the supervisor of the Purchase Invoice Department and the manager of the Treasurers Department. This was justified as a means of assembling a representative spread of contributors, rather than just a collection of the most popular members of staff. Yet the possible consequences of this, of selecting unpopular people, for example, or individuals who command little respect in the wider community, are not even considered. There is little sign of reflective management or sensitive engagement with the wider community on the composition and functioning of the design group.

Despite this conservative influence, the design group presented three options, ranging from job enrichment within the existing operational structure to multi-skilled teamworking for particular grades of staff and categories of activity. The more radical option, though preferred by the designers, was rejected by managers, and, after some pressure salesmanship, a watered-down version was accepted, which Henshall hopes will lead to his own preferred option in good time (Mumford and Henshall, 1979, p. 73). His favoured approach seems to tie precise numbers of staff to each team and involve the attendant elimination of the established grading scheme, an option that is considered too revolutionary for higher grades to accept in the first instance. This is hardly surprising given the implied loss of status, and possibly also remuneration.

This apparent interest in revisiting terms and conditions of employment as part of the participation process passes without any independent comment from Mumford or her supporters in the research community. Without any hint of irony, the Mumford and Henshall text reports that senior figures never imposed any constraints on the design group or intervened in a negative manner:

> The role of senior management through their membership of the Steering Group was both helpful and liberating (Mumford and Henshall, 1979, p. 105).

> The Steering Group's advice enabled the Design Group to free itself from a too timid approach to the redesign of work (Mumford and Henshall, 1979, p. 106).

> Without encouragement from the Steering Group, the Design Group might have been too conservative in its approach (Mumford and Henshall, 1979, p. 27).

The apparent failure to detect any difficulties with this situation begs some fundamental questions about the putative safeguards and participative credentials of socio-technical practice. While the Scandinavian researchers would be looking for trade union involvement under these circumstances, the ETHICS accounts offer nothing at all under the heading 'union versions'.

In the Mumford and Henshall text, a book of 190 pages, the question of union involvement is dismissed with a few bland words of appreciation in the preface. This treatment may seem entirely justified, since union officials made only guest appearances and the lone representative on the steering committee was absent when Mumford and the managers decided how the project was to proceed (p. 18). Critical reflection offers another possibility, however. Union figures could have been reading the situation with a more acute sense of micro politics, running for cover at the thought of being embroiled in any challenge to approved grading systems.

The failure to recognise the difficulties with this case, and the persistence in presenting it as an exemplary episode, seriously undermines the case for an ETHICS-based activism. This is a matter of theory and conceptualisation, of obscuring rather than illuminating the problematics of participation. No matter how skilfully constructed the methodology, or elegantly defended, theoretical sensitivity is required to target factors that inhibit progress, that are experienced as limiting or constraining at close quarters by those involved. It is not enough merely to condemn token participation, or to acknowledge the risks of manipulation without the social realism to recognise and tackle it in practice. Despite the references to critical reflection and broader social theory, there is nothing in the ETHICS package that permits an effective analysis of the impact that status differences, organisational hierarchies and established control systems can have upon the process. The interplay between organisational structures, cultures and the conduct of participation projects is conceptualised in abstract and unrealistically consensual terms. Hence, the judgement offered by the Scandinavian critics is well founded. To the extent that local worries and reported constraints remain out of focus, Hirschheim and Klein's reformulation fails to release ETHICS from its conservative influence.

STRUCTURES AND STRUGGLES

Alternative, less promotional survey and case material (Beirne and Ramsay, 1988, 1992; Beath and Orlikowski, 1994; Howcroft and Wilson, 2003) illustrates the typical obstacles and the degree of difficulty that confronts those who would seriously strive to achieve participative design. Constraints on the prospects for more open collaboration are located within established hierarchies, institutional settings and cultural contexts, including professional affiliations and the continuing influence of rationalistic frames of reference. The net result is a far less cheerful picture of the practice of user participation to date, and of the patterns of intervention necessary to secure more progressive formats in the future.

Counteracting the attractive socio-technical image of unambiguous and relatively painless user empowerment, the findings from these studies reveal the importance of authority relations, the reproduction of hierarchy and the lingering defence of decision-making prerogatives by managerial grades from both operational and information systems spheres of influence. The outcome is that elaborate structures of participation operate to frame the exchanges between the various stakeholders in each technology process, affecting and often restricting their contributions.

Design projects in practice typically work on a separation of issues, distinguishing aspects that are worthy of user collaboration from others that are decidedly non-negotiable or participatory. This is reinforced by complex arrangements that fragment and formalise the process, incorporating users selectively according to protocols, prerogatives, and occasionally the whims of specialists and more senior others. Hence the discovery that user participation is typically splintered by grade, status and stage of development, with only a very small proportion of available users experiencing any kind of sustained involvement in design activities (Beirne and Ramsay, 1988, 1992).

Considering the composition of user groups, survey data from the 1980s suggests that middle and senior managers have the closest involvement, contributing to 55 per cent and 46 per cent of schemes respectively (Beirne and Ramsay, 1988). Lower managerial and clerical staff experienced curtailed contact, the latter having an input to only 37 per cent of the schemes identified at that time. Involvement by secretarial and manual workers was a fleeting and minority activity, apparent in just 4 per cent of reported cases, and showing little sign of expansion according to more recent reports (Howcroft and Wilson, 2003). To make matters worse, there are peaks and troughs of participation for particular categories of user through the distinct phases of the technology process. Non-managerial white-collar workers are predominantly involved, if at all, in the work analysis, implementation and operational adjustment phases of any project. Shop floor workers are marginalized to an even greater extent, with far lower numbers involved though at similar points. This picture contrasts sharply with reported socio-technical episodes, suggesting that participation is seriously restricted in practice, limiting the contribution that knowledgeable people can make.

These conclusions are bolstered by case study evidence that provides additional depth to supplement the profile information from available surveys (Beirne and Ramsay, 1992; Howcroft and Wilson, 2003). This fills out the detail of a typically fragmented and divided process, even among developers, the experts formally credited with driving and controlling progress. Although technologists and users are often treated as homogeneous groups, the case evidence reveals a differentiated pattern of multiple team involvement, with extensive filtering and tiering of user and expert contributions along conventional lines of authority.

Users, for their part, are selectively incorporated according to their position and status, rather than their knowledge *per se*. It is common to find a clustering of users from similar grades and levels in the employment ladder (Beirne and Ramsay, 1992). The time that each group devotes to development matters, the steps at which it occurs and the influence achieved depends very much on the member's existing position within formal decision-making structures. Involvement therefore proceeds by way of an elaborate division of labour.

Senior executives form strategic planning teams that have high levels of discretion though short spans of participation, dealing mainly with the priorities and direction of each development. Beneath this level of strategic decision-making there are various management teams, ranging from quite senior standing committees responsible for steering, planning and budgeting decisions to junior advisory councils and work groups that are convened for a specific purpose at a particular stage of development. Computing professionals are involved in all of these, though again the hierarchy within the information systems or management services department has a bearing on the level of interaction with users. Senior computing professionals have formal responsibility for organising and managing user contributions. Systems analysts and front-line computing workers deal mainly with lower managerial and shop floor users on *ad hoc* involvement committees that are assembled during each of the key stages mentioned above.

For junior managerial and shop floor staff, this structuring of their involvement delivers a restricted and controlled experience. Despite the heavy emphasis or 'spin' that project managers commonly put on user participation, they are acutely aware that computing professionals are acting as gatekeepers on their input, 'picking their brains' during systems analysis or trying to head off resistance when it comes to implementation. They sense that their contribution is contained within narrow boundaries, and by the terms on which participation takes place (Beirne and Ramsay, 1992; Howcroft and Wilson, 2003).

This evidence highlights the very partial progress of user participation in practice, and the prevalence of shallow conceptions of user roles and authority. While proponents variously advocate engagement and emancipation, prevailing wisdom on how the process should be structured and managed effectively dilutes the experience, imposing familiar restrictions and conventions (Beath and Orlikowski, 1994). It seems that here, as elsewhere, participation is a resource that is used selectively by decision-makers to tackle particular problems in a manner that is consistent with their overall approach to employee relations. The lingering commitment to hierarchy, and to rationalistic management traditions generally within organisations, coincides with a strong professional attachment to technical divisions of labour, clear prerogatives and top-down design within the computing community.

Senior systems and user managers are often quite happy to endorse this, offering candid comments about their orientation (Beirne and Ramsay, 1992; Beirne *et al.*, 1998b). Far from welcoming progressive or extensive participation, a high proportion of them (especially those managing large departments or working for major employers) see it as destabilising, undermining the rigour of development practices and storing up employee relations problems for the future. Retaining a conventional engineering approach, they favour a minimum interaction model of involvement, targeting and monitoring user input through formal quality assurance arrangements. They also aim to tighten the control of technical staff, bringing them within more explicit hierarchical and bureaucratic management systems, and subjecting them to 'performance metrics' and monitoring tools that can differentiate fast from slow computing workers, for example. Sanctions have even been applied to developers who have overstepped their authority on user contact, with written warnings and reprimands issued to those who have acted on informal contact, making changes or correcting systems errors without going through approved channels (Beirne *et al.*, 1998b).

This evidence magnifies the difficulties surrounding participative systems development. For all the laudable sentiments in the research literature, the usual practice of participation has little to do with empowering users or conceding any independent influence over development decisions. The good intentions and innovative interventions proposed by enthusiasts therefore need to be evaluated against real world obstacles and constraints, including the capacity of conservative interests to defend or modify conventional practice. Realism should not be equated with determinate or inevitably debilitating outcomes, however. Rationalistic inclinations do not in themselves guarantee results, either on the imposition of process controls or the delivery of effective technology. Recalling the relational theory of power and political interaction from Chapter 1, it is also important to map out the space for struggle and progressive action, recognising that rationalistic attempts to structure and control user participation do not exhaust the possibilities or even attract universal approval among senior figures.

In common with broader accounts of unfettered managerial control over employees, images of passive involvement can obscure the contested nature of organisational relations. There is evidence that users 'see through' narrow conceptualisations, and are often very adept at creating space for themselves and contriving more positive roles, despite significant difficulties (Beirne *et al.*, 1998a). Just as rationalistic strategies have met resistance from workers in other areas, so users and developers have acted against rationalistic computing design. There are examples of grassroots activity beneath the surface of structured methods, with bank staff and engineering workers taking the initiative to defeat monitoring functions, penetrate security screens and disable productivity controls (Salzman and Rosenthal, 1994). Perhaps more surprisingly, there is evidence of users acting to improve systems performance, intervening 'after the fact' of top-down design to make them workable.

Clement (1993, 1994) and Nardi and Miller (1991) explain how clerical workers are able to adapt generic software packages on an incremental basis to make them useful for their own work, establishing spreadsheet templates, constructing databases and devising word processing conventions. These workers extend development processes beyond formal 'sign offs' and completion arrangements, accomplishing de facto design tasks on their own terms.

One of the most striking examples of this informal, yet very direct, user influence was discovered at a Scottish further education college (Beirne *et al.*, 1998a). Staff employed on short-term contracts to input data to a new, though seriously flawed, student records system redefined their job boundaries to include programming and development work, securing positive results which eluded in-house project managers and the contracted suppliers of the application software. Two users who had some computing training were particularly creative, experimenting with unfamiliar query languages and, through trial and error, devising a way of delivering useful reports to administrators, lecturers and senior managers. These de facto designers were motivated by a sense of disenchantment with the pressures they were confronting in their work, and which they eventually felt compelled to tackle by overstepping the terms of their employment contracts. They informally reskilled themselves, with the tacit backing of the college authorities after news spread about their effectiveness. While stressing that their activities were unofficial and 'on their own heads', senior figures turned a 'blind eye', even paying for them to attend training courses at a local university to refine their illicit skills.

This case provides an insight into the fundamental and sometimes subtle social processes that affect the development of work technology. In this respect, it counteracts the influence of over-rationalised prescriptions and formalised models of the technology process. Yet the informal interventions and concessions that characterised this episode occurred within a structural context. They were enacted within a managerial regime where enthusiasm for more direct control, and frustration at its elusiveness, were nonetheless readily apparent. There was a ceiling on managerial approval. This was informed partly by rationalistic leanings, but also by traditional orientations that are familiar from other work contexts. The divisions and demarcations in this case clearly reflected gender dynamics, a feature that exacerbated the constraints and contradictions in the process, generating tensions that eventually took their toll on some of the key people involved (Beirne *et al.*, 1998a).

The data entry workers here, as in many other information systems settings, were female, their managers male. Eventually, the two key users found themselves in a more directive environment with male systems managers appointed above them. Although keen to develop their own roles, and initially confident that their proven creativity would be acknowledged through more secure terms of employment, senior managers seemed eager to forget about this user-driven reality, and to install a more conventionally 'safe' set of arrangements. Ultimately, they were uncomfortable with the achievements of their user designers, feeling obliged to restrict grassroots influence and even take decisions that adversely affected the employment situation of the shop floor staff. The female systems workers in this case lost the advantages of their informal role in terms of skill development, job satisfaction and sense of achievement as their methods were officialised. They also experienced personal slights and difficulties in dealing with management as the new appointments and controls took effect, and the dilution of their own contribution was justified to them. This raises broader issues about the agenda for progressive management, extending the focus of critical reflection to include a richer mix of cultural and sub-cultural forces and prevailing patterns of socialisation.

4. Culture, management and innovation

While much of the interest in advancing employee empowerment has been channelled into technical arrangements – redefining job structures and changing skill content, layout and workspace design – mixed reactions and tensions between rival interpretations have drawn attention to subjectivity and culture as crucial aspects of innovation. As previous chapters have established, front-line accounts of empowerment are pluralistic, covering a range of meanings and reflecting different readings, interests and orientations. Regardless of sector and setting, large numbers of people, managers and employees, remain to be convinced about the merits and practicalities of empowerment. A sense of caution underpins even favourable evaluations, while negative judgements point to fragmentary, temporary or contradictory outcomes. Reactions to the same scheme often range from measured approval to complaints from some 'empowered' staff that the experience reproduced rather than transformed their sense of inequality, injustice or disadvantage.

The stance that different people adopt has much to do with their underlying values and established ways of thinking, feeling and sense-making. Particular views and ways of reading and engaging with organisational events 'live on' through innovative episodes, filtering and influencing them as they unfold from a sense of the past. This means that structural interventions are mediated through habitual and traditional ways of living and coping with a dynamic world. For all the attention given to structures and the technical apparatus of empowerment, the fortunes of practical programmes are crucially dependent on cultural and sub-cultural influences.

This chapter takes an in-depth look at culture and subjectivity, evaluating their significance for the empowerment project and considering how they simultaneously impinge upon, and develop from, patterns of innovation. In terms of the conceptual framework explained at the outset and developed through previous chapters, the point here is to accommodate cultural dimensions explicitly and effectively within a relational understanding of power, struggle and practice.

PRESCRIPTIONS FOR CULTURAL CHANGE

The mixed reactions of those affected by empowerment programmes are often difficult for prescriptive management theorists and consultants to take. For this group, they signify an unhealthy or wrong-headed fixation with outmoded values and the legacy of the past. There is a frustration, at least in part of the management literature, with deeply embedded cultural characteristics, specifically the top-down ethos and authoritarianism that Taylorism and Fordism nurtured more than a century ago, and which continue to exert a millstone influence on modern practitioner thinking (Peters and Waterman, 1982; Kanter, 1984; Deal and Kennedy, 1999).

From here, too many people are locked into 'them and us' values and priorities, to a 'command and control' logic that threatens to destabilise any gains that can be achieved with the restructuring of work. This necessitates a rather more fundamental challenge to the way that people think about empowerment and innovation. Measures that target job structures may be solid and sensible given current competitive conditions yet are liable to fail when fastened to organisations that cherish the values of the old industrial order. By this reasoning, the promise of empowerment is to be realized not so much by altering structures but winning hearts and minds. Innovation becomes a cultural as much as a structural intervention. It means changing the corporate ethos, the core values, attitudes and beliefs that influence behaviour, socialising people into the role of 'team players' and overcoming any ingrained tendency towards low-trust, adversarial relations.

This is very much a product of the excellence tradition of the 1980s, a movement that was stimulated by the publication of Peters and Waterman's book *In Search of Excellence* (1982) and fuelled by the pronouncements of like-minded consultants and management gurus who were eager to jettison any cultural baggage that inhibited performance (Deal and Kennedy, 1982; Robson, 1988). At a time of industrial upheaval and dislocation, when many Western companies were coming to terms with the economic ascendancy of their Japanese competitors, this case for cultural renewal struck a chord with prominent executives and senior managers, notably in the car industry and in consumer electronics (Starkey and McKinlay, 1994). The success of Japanese manufacturers seemed to underline the significance of common values and a consensual approach to work organisation. These companies were evidently adding value to their structural arrangements by enlisting the help and co-operation of their people in a purposeful, family-like fashion (Pascale and Athos, 1986).

The putative virtues of homogeneous values and the consensual Japanese corporation may be less compelling since the Asian economic crises of 1998 and 1999 revealed tensions, when admired innovators such as Nissan and

Mazda were dismantling the 'golden principles' of job and contract security and staff welfare provision (BBC, 2000). However, in the context of the 1980s, these were potent symbols in the campaign for 'strong' cultures and 'turned on' corporate citizens. Politicians and wider interest groups were also reinforcing the message, expressing policy initiatives in cultural terms and, most obviously in Britain, associating renewal with prosperity under the banner of an 'enterprise culture'.

Not that employer attempts to influence culture originated during this period. When faced with problems of absenteeism and labour turnover in the early twentieth century, Henry Ford had tried to manipulate working class values so that staff would be more inclined to accept the pressures of his harsh regime. Various measures were devised, from bonus schemes to an Americanisation programme for immigrants, all of them aiming to move people on an emotional and patriotic level, to 'help' them internalise Ford's vision of an appropriate work ethic and instil a greater collective sense of efficiency and industrial discipline (Littler and Salaman, 1984; Ford and Crowther, 1926).

As it was portrayed in the 1980s, however, culture management was a more seductive and seemingly neutral (less ethically charged) prospect, the excellence gurus investing it with an elixir-like potential to transform the fortunes of ailing companies (Thompson and McHugh, 1995; Collins, 2000). Cultural change became the solution to organisational ills. It was, and still is, prescribed as an antidote to the effects of disparate thinking and behaviour, an essential way of uniting corporate citizens behind irreproachable goals (Deal and Kennedy, 1982, 1999). The resulting mantra is that excellent companies thrive because they engage in restructuring while at that same time enthusing people to be co-operative and creative. Their 'change masters' (Kanter, 1984) simultaneously humanise structures and 'unfreeze' the status quo, decentralising work arrangements while creating a culture that is conducive to the change.

Yet in this project, culture carries a very specific meaning. It is the product of management decision-making, an expression of the way that senior figures define the character and purpose of an organisation. It is, in other words, the official view, the sense of itself that is generated from the top, or as Deal and Kennedy (1982) more (in)famously put it, 'the way we do things around here'. Culture is the 'higher cause' that glues the various communities of organisational life together (Deal and Kennedy, 1999), the 'software of the mind' (Hofstede, 1991) or 'collective mental programming' (Schein, 1985) that connects people to organisational goals.

Executives are told that to nurture innovation, this 'hot wiring' must privilege humanistic concerns, putting people first and foremost on the corporate agenda. The lesson drawn from excellent companies is that supportive cultures gather strength by expressing anti-authoritarian sentiments, demonstrating a concern for employee welfare and cultivating a reciprocal identification with the needs of the organisation. On this reading, shared values are established by driving fear out of the workplace and creating an atmosphere of openness, trust and cohesion (Peters and Waterman, 1982; Deal and Kennedy, 1999).

So how does an organisation develop and solidify this strong culture of mutual care and concern? For most of these authors, and certainly the more consultancy-minded commentators (including Martin and Nicholls, 1987; Roth, 1997; Ward, 1996; Nicholls, 1995), the process is reasonably straightforward. As a first step, transformational leaders are charged with creating a clear vision and corresponding 'umbrella of beliefs' (Deal and Kennedy, 1999), mining company history for suitable signals, benchmarking elements of this against admired organisations, and ensuring that the final package is consistent with the environment and characteristics of the business or service. Procedures, rituals and ceremonies are then devised to 'summon the collective spirit'. Corporate symbols are created and a distinctive language contrived to engender feelings of identification and shared mission.

Inspirational leadership is at the centre of the process. All of the main gurus agree that the ability of an organisation to be culturally progressive is crucially dependent on enlightened leaders who have a clear vision of how to put people first, and a determination to follow through, 'walking the walk and talking the talk' (Deal and Kennedy, 1999). With such a thrusting and dynamic image of leadership roles at the heart of the recipe, it is perhaps unsurprising that a large population of senior executives appear to have taken the advice. There are many examples of corporate 'change masters' rehearsing the case for cultural renewal, and attaching their personal seal of approval to moulding and socialising programmes (Robson, 1988; Jones, 2000; McCabe, 2002). Yet their efforts reveal a remarkable sameness and monotony of practice.

The imprint of the guru schemes is discernible in all sorts of initiatives and settings, with their vocabulary and measures reproduced to a standard format. The Values Framework at the BBC is similar to the Visions and Values scheme at Collins publishing, which is much the same as the Hewlett-Packard Way, the Microsoft Way and the Scottish Power statement of 'commandments' setting out what it will and will not do. These organisations, like many others, are keen to present their people-friendly credentials for attention, to project cohesive cultural characteristics and exemplify progressive leadership. Their web sites and promotional documents, both for internal and external consumption, proclaim that their purpose is to enrich the lives of staff and clients, to be creative at whatever they do, to build trust and respect with integrity and genuine conviction.

These claims about their essence, what they stand for and represent, are typically reinforced with policies and procedures, symbols and imagery that attempt to make the message convincing. The details are usually modelled on arrangements associated with the showcase organisations and exemplary cultures on Peters and Waterman's original list, reaching back to IBM, Disney, Hewlett-Packard and others. The efforts of these 'pioneering' companies in packaging and presenting their mission, translating it into dress codes, logos and corporate jargon, connecting it to stories and legends about charismatic founders and heroic managers are absorbed and replicated.

Human resource programmes aim to induct people deliberately and often elaborately into the life of the organisation, cultivating their commitment through subsequent performance appraisal and development programmes that re-emphasise values and expectations. Work locations are designed and coloured to reflect humanistic concerns, to be ergonomically pleasing and conducive to a positive experience, with windows and views or rest areas, rather than regimented cubicles and ill-considered lighting that contributes to a sense of drudgery. Walls are decorated with posters and slogans that help people to feel proud of their organisation, to identify with the pronouncements of their leaders, share in their hopes for the future and recognise that they are valued members of an inclusive community.

Clearly, these measures are introduced with the intention of fusing people together, of moulding and socialising their commitment so that they welcome innovation, responding positively on a consensual basis and without the disruptive influence of fractured judgements about its significance. Whether culture is really amenable to such managerial shaping is a matter of intense controversy, however.

For some people in the research community and within organisations, culture management constitutes a potent force. The recipe targets the emotions of managers and workers in a way that renders them more susceptible to the pronouncements and priorities of senior figures. Without really being conscious of the effects, by some accounts, their identity begins to merge with the interests of the organisation. They surrender a greater part of themselves and their independent influence as they become equivalent to 'Beamers' at IBM (Willmott, 1993).

For others, the formula is simply too crude, trite and faddish, with little or no substance to command serious attention. A large number of reviews are caustic and dismissive. *In Search Of Excellence* has been savaged in recent years, critics finding plenty of ammunition in the performance figures subsequently delivered by companies on the list, and the dramatic fall from grace of American 'institutions' like IBM. It was described as 'the epitome of eighties shallowness' in *Business Age* magazine, 'a book for juveniles' (by Drucker, quoted in Silver, 1987), and 'dead wrong' by agents of the United States Justice Department (DeLamarter, 1988).

Others again complain that culture has been commercialised by this treatment, that something valuable has been lost through accounts that reduce it to a corporate resource or communication device. By this reading, the culture management movement is at best a red herring, or worse, a disruptive influence that has stifled analysis and applied research, deflecting attention from richer source material that can help to clarify key concepts and contextualise innovation.

CRITICAL EVALUATIONS

The main worry for some critics is that culture management succeeds. They fear that it may limit and contain human experience, raising disturbing questions about distortion, manipulation and the servicing of elite interests. Some find it offensive, equating cultural change programmes with subjugation, the insidious control of subjectivity and nascent totalitarianism (Willmott, 1993; Grey, 1994; Ray, 1986). From here, culture begins to blend with surveillance as employees internalise the values of the organisation to the point where they police their own activities, and management control is exercised through worker self-discipline. Smith and Wilkinson (1996) detect such an outcome at Sherwoods, a company that ostensibly followed the prescriptive guidelines enthusiastically with integrative, non-authoritarian initiatives that delivered harmony and zealous conformity on management terms. By this evidence, culture management is a warped and malevolent project, a variation on Taylorism and Fordism and not, as publicised, the key to a humanistic alternative. It caters for elite interests, dominating rather than empowering, overwhelming instead of respecting people and their contributions.

This literature offers a potent antidote to upbeat managerialism. It provides an effective inducement to critical thinking and even a sceptical disposition, which is healthy when confronting the positive claims made for management recipes and 'universal' solutions in this area, as in others. However, there are grounds for caution, and for applying critical scrutiny to this bleak interpretation of culture management. In fact, there is a close correspondence between this treatment of culture and the stance taken by some of the critical writers on power and managerialism that were reviewed in the first chapter. At that stage, the contrasts between resource models, or capacity-outcome views, of power were found to be less significant than the similarities between them, which deflected attention away from relations of interdependence. The same applies to the analytical divisions between these opposing accounts of culture management. The critics share some key conceptual difficulties with the authors they seek to challenge.

Culture is more complex than either account permits. By concentrating on strength and control, integration and uniformity, consensus and value-internalisation, they oversimplify the subjectivities, processes and uncertainties involved. The most telling critiques of culture management point to the impossibility of creating truly uniform corporate cultures, and the limited effect of identity-building and symbolic conditioning measures of the sort advocated by the gurus. This is not to suggest that culture is beyond influence. On the contrary, the point is to promote a dynamic appreciation of culture, connecting it to a relational understanding of power and interaction as a feature of life that is continually negotiated rather than malleable and determinate.

The fearful view of culture management sides with the gurus in assuming that leaders are capable of creating culture. In this respect, both camps overstate their case. They work with an impression of senior executives that is unrealistic. As some other authors have noted (Thompson and McHugh, 1995; Collins, 2000), they seem to be taken in by the image of themselves that prominent executives and corporate personalities often cultivate, as 'masters of the universe' who command allegiance and preside over cohesive entities that have been forged in their own image. Their accounts differ mainly on the motives, ethics and interests that are attributed to these able and focused leaders.

Yet those at the top of organisational hierarchies have never been able to wield such authority, or to marginalize other interests and influences to the point where they become irrelevant to the nature and understanding of everyday events. The images traded by the gurus, and by this constituency of critical commentators, exaggerate the capabilities of corporate leaders, and also the receptiveness (or gullibility) of the managers and staff who operate below them in the official pecking order. No matter how charismatic, focused or active they may be in deploying the prescriptive techniques of culture management, leaders are simply unable to exert a totalising influence on culture. Accounts that suggest otherwise crucially ignore both the strength and diversity of interests and affiliations that influence organisational life.

Workplace behaviour is variously framed, inspired and constrained by a complex mix of values, orientations and attachments, many of them transcending organisational boundaries. Members of work organisations are typically drawn from different geographical areas, social classes, sexes, ethnic groups and religions. These aspects of existence are not suspended or removed when people pass through the gates of their employing organisation. They inevitably approach their work in a way that reflects their upbringing, early socialisation and wider life experiences, blending these together with occupational and professional influences, and others from within the organisation, including those from hierarchical, functional and specialist associations.

References to a uniform, all-embracing and monolithic corporate culture are difficult to sustain when this level of diversity is called into the analysis. These 'other' influences cannot be said to operate beyond, underneath or alongside the official culture because they interlock with it in a dynamic and often unpredictable manner. As Fincham and Rhodes (1992, p. 420) effectively phrase it, they 'form the basis of distinctive sub-cultures and counter-cultures that compete to define the reality of the organisation'. Despite the efforts of the corporate culture gurus and their prominent followers, organisations are multicultural. They consist of various constellations of values and impulses that sometimes overlap or coincide, occasionally clash, and at other times exert a more subtle influence on events. This multicultural mix ensures that a large population is involved in framing the nature and identity of an organisation. It is not an attribute of leadership or something that lies within the gift of executives, no matter how enlightened their approach.

A number of writers have underlined the importance of workplace sub-cultures, establishing their potential for influence, explaining how this is reproduced and pointing to their resilience (Roy, 1973; Jones, 2000; Eastman and Fulop, 1997). Informal behaviour patterns and experiences with esoteric language figure prominently in accounts of cultural processes, especially those that flourish unofficially or in spite of management opposition. During the course of their work, individuals encounter forms of banter, humour and behavioural regularities that reinforce existing sub-cultures and counter-cultures. These are initially filtered and interpreted through norms and values that have already been assimilated, and which make the surrounding events seem more or less sensible, perhaps shocking, irrelevant and pointless, or possibly just a variation on taken-for-granted aspects of social engagement. People respond in a way that reflects their personal history and the constraints of the situation, gravitating towards some affiliations while spurning others with varying degrees of diplomacy. Yet the emerging pattern of association, affiliation, tolerance and avoidance is fluid and dynamic rather than consciously settled. Multicultural influences are subject to negotiation over time and in light of experience, resisting definitive classification or rational separation into categories that either support or challenge officialdom (Hatch, 1997).

In fact, people are capable of expressing distinctly different and seemingly contradictory values, of identifying with competing sub-cultures on an everyday basis. Jones (2000) provides a telling example from his personal experience of employment with work-study engineers at a Hotpoint domestic appliance factory in North Wales. He was assigned to a small group of some fifteen individuals who shared a Taylorist outlook on work roles and formal relationships, exhibiting a mutual intolerance for operator slacking, which they regarded as a key management issue, and by extension a collective allegiance to machine pacing and work measurement as vital means of maintaining control. Yet these engineers had multiple identities, some of them based around sports, drinking and music that contributed to sub-cultures that straddled Taylorist demarcation lines between 'them and us'. There were regular patterns of social interaction between the engineers and shop floor workers that had a bearing upon exchanges between them. Although these engineers were part of a sub-culture that disparaged and fostered conflict with operators, some of them had established another identity as 'one of the boys'.

By this reckoning, the lines of influence between affiliation and expression are occasionally surprising, though seldom straightforward. Yet enthusiasts for culture management continue to present a unifying agenda based on programming from the top. Where sub-cultures are acknowledged, in the second of Deal and Kennedy's books, for example, discussion centres on the management challenge of 'knitting them together', of creating 'umbrella beliefs to unite disparate subcultures…into a coherent and cohesive whole' (1999, p. 203). The assumption that leaders can apply the chosen message and appeal to people over and above other influences and orientations persists. An abundance of empirical evidence now supports the theoretical case for dismissing this proposition, however.

The work-study engineers at Hotpoint were able to maintain their sense of purpose and relevance, and indeed their capacity to exert an influence on work organisation, despite a cultural change programme that explicitly challenged their position (Jones, 2000). The arrival of a new managing director marked a watershed in official thinking about work and employee relations, with 'humanistic' innovations introduced and traditional Tayloristic ideas openly criticised. Here was a new management regime with focused believers who were apparently putting the recipe for cultural renewal to work.

Time studies and stopwatch measurements were rejected as techniques that were 'demeaning to operators', and a payment-by-results scheme dismantled on the grounds that it encouraged 'sloppy work'. Yet their subjective sense of management priorities and necessary behaviour moved the work-study group to resist, and to carry on regardless of the signals and initiatives from above. They held on to the belief that productivity levels were modest, that worker discretion would be taken as a licence for slacking, and that the leadership line had not really been thought through or related to operational conditions at their factory.

Crucially, the subjectivities that sustained the work-study sub-culture were reinforced rather than undermined by the changes because the self-image of the engineers as custodians of efficiency actually hardened. On their terms, the new leaders had a poor grasp of management realities, and were governed by fashionable notions or misplaced idealism. They were the only managers with any real understanding of efficiency, so it was important for them collectively to sustain their commitment despite the regime, and until their contribution was verified or appreciated. This was an oppositional sub-culture that had been 'tightened' by the experience of culture management. Group members were highly sensitive to their engineering subjectivities, and more likely to spark conflict with workers and senior executives as a result.

Other case evidence registers similar doubts about managerial responsiveness, although highlighting different forms of resistance. Various researchers have called attention to distancing, acting and role-playing behaviour that enables people on the receiving end of culture management to counteract unpalatable or uncomfortable effects (Ogbonna and Wilkinson, 1990; Anthony, 1994; McCabe, 2002). There are reports of managers feeling exposed by the antics of leaders who stage-manage cultural events and launch quirky initiatives, and then expect them to rehearse embarrassing slogans and sell the 'concept' to staff. Many baulk at the gimmickry and 'novelty' of culture management, and feel uncomfortable with the clichéd language of innovation spouted by their leaders and imported by consultants.

For these managers, the apparatus of culture management is not intrinsically motivating or uplifting. Their identity and sense of self is challenged. Nonetheless, feelings of personal unease and the perception that credibility with staff is at risk have to be set against the expectation from above that policy will be implemented. Impression management is the answer for some, 'going through the motions', acting out roles for each constituency, and resorting to an older and more 'natural' discourse whenever possible (Ogbonna and Wilkinson, 1990; McCabe, 2002). These reactions signal something other than value internalisation. Managerial subjectivities here, as in the previous example, produce varied and competing lines of influence.

Counter-cultures are also discernible at leadership level. In fact, senior figures in companies that profess to have inclusive and progressive cultures have been widely criticised for not adhering to the officially cherished values, of 'not practising what they preach', of exhibiting sub-cultural tendencies of their own that contradict the corporate culture. The debates around financial participation and outcry in Britain about 'fat cat' salaries provide a useful illustration.

Financial participation is frequently associated with empowerment, partnership and innovation, attracting enthusiastic support from a cross-section of industrialists, politicians and trades unionists, especially in the form of employee share ownership schemes (Jenkins and Poole, 1990). Apart from the promise of financial gains for participants, the expansion of employee share ownership is endorsed as another means of promoting attitudinal change. In theory, because employees become part owners and draw dividend benefits from higher profitability, share schemes encourage co-operation, produce a closer identity of interests and a reduction in 'them and us' tensions between managers and workers (Baddon, *et al.*, 1989; Pendleton, 1995).

However, these benefits are by no means assured. Enthusiasts have struggled to convince people that schemes are effectively resourced, and that they operate in a fair and balanced way. Research evidence suggests that people are acutely aware of inequalities in company share programmes, recognising differences between the arrangements for employees and executives in terms of scale and capitalisation, discounts, options and acquisition plans, and the opportunities for reaping financial benefits (Baddon 1989; O'Connell-Davidson and Nichols, 1991). A steady flow of information through newspapers and reports, typically linked to editorials and condemnations of executive excess, has magnified this disparity (*Financial Times*, 2004; *Daily Record*, 2003; *Sunday Telegraph*, 1993).

The most common complaint against share schemes, and financial participation arrangements more generally, is that they fragment team behaviour, causing disappointment, disgruntlement and even resentment (*The Herald*, 1996; Pendleton, 1995). Inflated remuneration packages that favour executives with share options and other bonuses that are out of line with company performance or realised during periods of 'downsizing' and 'cut-backs' (Randle, 1997; *Scotland on Sunday*, 1999; Labour Research Department, 2002) have been sending signals about organisational values that are at odds with the vision set out by the culture gurus, and reproduced in corporate handbooks. They support images of sectionalism and elitism, rather than unity and cohesion.

Accusations of greed and hypocrisy have been heard by researchers and reported in the media, with employees and managers criticising what they regard as the 'do as I say and not as I do' sub-culture in some of Britain's major companies (*Scotland on Sunday*, 1999; *Daily Record*, 1998). Not surprisingly, perceptions about unfair practice and the divisiveness of schemes that seem to be 'rigged' in favour of executives have undermined declarations about openness, trust and shared values, reinforcing 'them and us' attitudes (Baddon, *et al.*, 1989; O'Connell-Davidson and Nichols, 1991; *The Herald*, 1996). The meanings that leaders have tried to shape through culture management have been influenced in fact by aspects of their personal and collective identities that are formally removed from the process yet attract subjective judgements from other constituents.

These examples demonstrate the vulnerability of imposed cultural change programmes and expose the limited grasp of theory and empirical evidence that informs a lot of prescriptive managerial and fearful critical commentary about cultural engineering and the moulding of human subjectivity. Executive influences on organisational culture are neither uniform nor decisive, exhibiting contrasting and even contradictory tendencies that are mediated by other subjectivities. This is something that senior figures in a growing list of companies that have followed the recipe are beginning to appreciate. The official rhetoric of their corporate culture is far removed from the everyday meanings and understandings captured by in-house attitude surveys and by independent research studies that have tracked staff reactions to culture shaping programmes (Thompson and Findlay, 1996). Significant investments of time, energy and resources have failed to impress, exacerbating tensions and raising the reported levels of dissatisfaction and distrust.

The British Airways slide from confident culture management to conflict, strife and managerial fire-fighting is one of the most dramatic and widely recognised. Despite many years of cultural conditioning from the 1980s, 'Putting People First', 'Managing People First, 'Visioning the Future', fostering pride and the service ethic through 'Customer First Teams' in the 'World's Favourite Airline' (Bruce, 1987; Robson, 1988; Hopfl *et al.*, 1992), members of staff were still forming and expressing their own views about company life, and these were persistently critical. The idealised view from the top was regularly punctured by grassroots experiences and understandings, backfiring quite spectacularly in the late 1990s during disputes with cabin crew and catering staff that exposed the less palatable propensities of key executives and functional managers.

New terms and conditions were imposed, cutting overtime, mileage and unsocial hours allowances, allocating some services to outside contractors, and introducing tighter controls and monitoring systems to improve staff performance. Accusations about intimidatory tactics and heavy-handed management captured headlines, and support from some unlikely sources. There was a general outcry about the 'shop-a-mate' money saving initiative that encouraged staff to blow the whistle on colleagues who were squandering or stealing resources (*Daily Record*, 1996). The British Medical Association complained to the company that a new requirement for staff to obtain a medical certificate for missing a single working day through ill health was unacceptable, placing significant burdens upon General Practitioners and asking them to be 'industrial policemen' (*The Guardian*, 1997b). Guidelines governing the height and weight of cabin staff attracted additional and very public criticism as pressure from within and beyond the company mounted on Chief Executive, Bob Ayling, to improve morale and service to customers (*Daily Record*, 1996; *The Guardian*, 1997a; *The Herald*, 1997).

This was all in stark contrast with the view of itself that the company sought to promote, and the irony was not lost on large numbers of frontline managers and employees (Hopfl *et al.*, 1992; *The Guardian* 1997a). Not that they were completely dismissive of the culture management initiatives. Some aspects were applauded and appreciated, though people were making discriminating judgements, seeing through the spin and calling upon wider and deeper reference points. For example, an event that was initiated in 1985 and entitled 'A Day in the Life' was credited by staff as offering a potentially useful means of cultivating participative awareness and respect for other contributions (Robson, 1988). Essentially, with this activity, representatives from different functional areas devised and delivered presentations, explaining what they do and claiming space for their role.

The wider significance of this was picked up and developed by administrators at an NHS staff development course hosted by the University of Glasgow in 1999. An acute sense of status differentials and frustration with elitism and hospital politics was translated into a campaign for fair treatment and mutual respect that had groups from porters and filing staff at medical records to managers, doctors and other professionals using a similar sort of approach to reflect on work roles and relationships. Back at British Airways, however, many employees were saddened that the scope for reflectively developing such helpful activities was overridden by more fundamental difficulties and tensions in employment relations.

CULTURE, STRUCTURE AND ARENAS OF STRUGGLE

Critical social science provides an important corrective to the culture management movement, bringing diversity sharply into focus and underlining the value of a relational approach. Clearly, culture is not a management resource. The cultural life of an organisation is collectively produced and reproduced by a wide range of constituents and in ways that are beyond management control. Yet framing and positioning people within contrasting and overlapping sub-cultures and patterns of socialisation does not by itself account for the dynamics of cultural formation, nor capture its significance for empowerment and innovation.

As emphasised in Chapter 1, the processes that enable people to derive meanings, to form interpretations and exercise judgement must be explicitly connected to structure, to the effects of markets, commerce and technology, for example. Culture and subjectivity cannot be separated out from the structural context in which meanings are produced and reproduced. The openness of subjectivity to local networks and sub-cultures, and to broader influences from upbringing, education, geography, gender, ethnicity, religion and so forth, should not deflect attention from the regularities of economy or the legal and institutional frameworks in which these processes are embedded (Beirne *et al.*, 2004).

It is necessary to consider the relational interdependencies between culture and structure, and to track their mutual influence on the inequalities and struggles that characterise organisational life. This is the dynamic context in which innovation occurs, develops, falters or fails. It is simultaneously fostered and constrained within arenas of struggle in which culture and subjectivity give meaning to, and at the same time reflect, structural tendencies.

Two recent studies exemplify this integrative treatment of empowerment and innovation. McCabe (2002) and Foster and Hoggett (1999) explain how dimensions of subjectivity connect with structural factors to influence innovation in particular arenas of struggle. Focusing on developments within an insurance company and at three branches of the British Benefits Agency, they demonstrate that correlations of culture and structure produce various coexisting and cross-cutting axes of struggle that reflect the past while reshaping it through innovative episodes, with results that are negotiated and often unanticipated, rather than given or pre-defined.

McCabe contextualises the subjectivities and struggles of middle to senior managers at AB Insurance during a period of departmental restructuring and computer-based job redesign. These developments were influenced by commercial concerns to improve quality and efficiency while reducing costs. Yet managerial and territorial sub-cultures were as important to the processes and outcomes of innovation as economics and technology.

The sectional interpretations, allegiances and promotional activities of three managers, of the Life Department, information technology and training, figure prominently in this analysis. Their respective expressions of contrasting and competing values, and attempts to secure personal status, identity and advantage, added impetus to internal politicking and manoeuvring as each tried to gain an edge and curry favour within the broader management community.

The Life Manager was steeped in the traditions of work-study that were ingrained within the company, and perpetuated through sub-cultural ties of the sort that Jones (2000) identified at Hotpoint. However, at AB Insurance, representatives of this sub-culture had risen through the ranks to formal positions that gave work-study values and preoccupations higher status and apparent credibility, conferring prestige upon those who were actively cutting costs, tightening controls and securing greater efficiencies. This manager was exemplifying these attitudes and concerns in his approach to innovation, and through this to career-building, pushing the technology programme towards work-tracking, task simplification and systems that would reduce the number of staff employed.

This reinforced political tensions and magnified some significant differences between AB sub-cultures. The IT Manager articulated concerns about a perceived challenge to the prerogatives, role and approach of the technology community, and was also moved to a personal defence of his identity and reputation for competence at senior levels as setbacks and technical difficulties were acknowledged and scrutinised. By contrast, the Training Manager adopted an offensive posture, attempting to bolster his status and identity by speaking to staff concerns about the employment effects of change, and highlighting the damaging impact of deskilling and disaffection on job performance.

As they engaged in the processes of navigating meanings and negotiating their positions, all three managers were constrained by broader managerial structures and subjectivities, however. Winning allies and mobilising support within the management hierarchy was crucial to their respective struggles, and this obliged them to observe other norms and inter-subjective realities. The Training Manager acknowledged that seeming to criticise work-study would be extremely damaging, and that pointing fingers or blaming colleagues for problems would be counterproductive. The patterns of struggle were even affected by language, with influence slipping through the use of terminology or by articulating a case that was perceived to be crass or outside of the established traditions of management expression.

Many of the managers and supervisors at AB were described as 'old school', promoted through the ranks for their diligence and knowledge of insurance, and holding on to a view of the company as paternalistic, genteel, respectable and stable. There was a shared antipathy towards novelty and managerial radicalism that had a bearing upon the struggles, and indeed was variously endorsed by the three managers since they had multiple identities, again as indicated by Jones (2000), straddling the sub-cultures noted above and the wider managerial community of which they were a part. McCabe (2002, p. 529) acknowledges the analytical significance of this, quoting Young (1989) to reinforce the message that 'unity and division exist in tandem', reflecting relational interdependencies, influencing struggles and the way that people interpret and act upon their situations.

Unfortunately, there is little in this account to indicate how the struggles at AB affected staff, or for that matter the fortunes of the Life, IT and Training Managers. In fairness, McCabe's priority was to account for processes rather than outcomes, to demonstrate that innovation is constituted through struggles that reflect particular cultural and structural contexts. Foster and Hoggett (1999) have more to say about the working through of alternative possibilities, about the interrelated effects of local labour markets and gendered office cultures on teamworking and empowerment at the Benefits Agency.

This research explains why proposals emanating from the centre of the organisation had very different local results. An empowerment programme that devolved staffing and budgetary responsibilities to middle and junior managers, encouraging them to provide an integrated 'one stop' service to clients via multidisciplinary teamworking, had a variable impact on struggles and patterns of organisation and management. The authors tracked developments at three offices within the same district. The first was located in a deprived inner-city area, the second in a more desirable part of the city centre, while the third was situated in a conservative seaside town. Although there were similarities in terms of the initial scepticism and concerns expressed by staff at each office, there were also significant differences, notably in labour market conditions, the physical layout of buildings and local office cultures.

Collaborative teamworking was only really endorsed and developed at the out-of-city branch, where there was clear evidence that previous demarcation lines between tasks, relationships and working areas had been altered, and that groups of people were sharing knowledge, skills and the same office space to cover a wider range of issues affecting each claimant. The researchers attribute this to the interrelated effects of structure and culture on local struggles. They point specifically to working ties and managerial sensitivities that were influenced by steady staffing under a depressed local labour market, a predominantly female workforce drawn from the surrounding community and with commitments that made the Agency's flexible working arrangements attractive, and also a Cinderella identity founded on perceptions that staff at other branches treated them as the poor relations in this particular district.

Not that this was a settled situation, or that the struggles behind multi-disciplinary teamworking had run their course. Tensions were discernible, when some of the younger women expressed sub-cultural concerns about a status-hierarchy based on age, for example. Nonetheless, when the research was conducted, the members of staff at this office generally acknowledged the benefits of an approach to innovation that their counterparts in the city dismissed as impracticably radical. Hostilities to multi-skilling and multi-disciplinary working were pronounced (though not uniform) at the other sites, where the respective combinations of place, labour market and counter-cultures had a contrasting influence on struggles and outcomes. The city centre branch had developed 'co-located' teams, where clusters of specialists worked in greater proximity to each other. By contrast, the office in the deprived area was firmly attached to specialisation, maintaining established boundaries with only very focused and informal teamworking among counter staff, who saw it as more of a support network for dealing with hostile claimants.

These studies conceptualise innovation as a variable quality of interdependent relations and cross-cutting struggles, embedding it within particular cultural and structural contexts. Clearly, managers and others are constantly orienting and reorienting themselves to unfolding processes, deriving meanings and interpreting events, with constrained options for acting, intervening and struggling. At one level, this underlines the problematics of empowerment and progressive intervention. Enthusiasts, and other actors, are caught up in dynamic arenas of struggle that are beyond personal influence and expressions of choice, commitment or inclination. Established structures, cultures and subjectivities inform and shape these struggles, yet are simultaneously reshaped and reconstituted as they unfold. This helps to explain why practical episodes are rarely as radical as the prescriptive gurus suggest, although it also negates the continuity case rehearsed by critics who dismiss empowerment as a gloss on given inequalities of influence and ownership.

Again, the dynamic processes of organisational struggle and exchange variously reproduce and transform workplace relations and experiences in ways that resist prior design, that present unanticipated challenges and deliver unintended consequences. They simultaneously generate constraints on progressive intervention and opportunities for creative engagement, stimulating awareness and opening up conditions for reflective practice. As McCabe notes at the end of his analysis (McCabe, 2000, p.533), the context of innovation provides an outlet for progressive thinking as well as the mobilisation of conservative concerns, providing a reason and creating scope for those who are moved by the broader principles empowerment and workplace reform to intervene.

PART TWO

Support structures and reflective practice

5.   Sustaining a voluntary commitment

The research reported in previous chapters demonstrates that empowerment is a highly charged, often fraught and inherently problematical process. Taking a panoramic view of the evidence, it is difficult to avoid the conclusion that progress towards any sort of authentic empowerment has been hesitant, and subject to frequent back-sliding and deterioration. We are not, as citizens and members of organisations, cumulatively better off as a result of either the recurring interest in direct participation or the broad range of supposedly empowering initiatives that have been introduced.

Many companies that claim to empower employees in practice do nothing of the sort. There is evidence of window dressing and appearance management, with lots of schemes in various contexts favouring rhetoric over substance. They offer an impression that progressive management is at work, yet fail seriously to challenge, or regularly slip back to, more conventional values and command structures. Hopes have often been raised and then dashed, while legitimate concerns have been dismissed out of hand. From their own experiences, a large number of managers and employees consider empowerment schemes to be hollow or unpalatable, variously expressing scepticism, cynicism, frustration and distrust. As previously discussed, the legacy of the past remains potent, generating significant obstacles and constraints. To paraphrase an oft-quoted remark by Tom Burns from the 1970s, the workplace continues to be one of the most authoritarian environments in democratic society.

Yet there is a danger of slipping from this sort of sober assessment to debilitating pessimism, and even negativity. The accumulated evidence of restricted or curtailed participation needs to be set against some recognised benefits, even if their impact to date has been sectional or fleeting. The sharp end evaluations that were reviewed through earlier chapters point to valued aspects and positive features, although judgements tend to be cautious, acknowledging that favourable outcomes are unevenly distributed, and by no means straightforward or secure.

There was also evidence of creative thinking, of innovative ideas and techniques, many of them devised by principled managers and workers who are collectively pushing the boundaries of possibility for meaningful change. There were solid proposals for structuring work in new and liberating ways, perhaps most obviously within Volvo. There was evidence of fresh thinking about viable ways of challenging sectionalism and elitism, including the 'Day in the Life' scenario at British Airways, which lends itself to a less dogmatic application than culture management, as argued in the last chapter. These developments highlight opportunities as well as constraints, useful lines of influence as well as dilemmas. They show that empowerment is potentially progressive, a worthwhile if struggle-suffused pursuit. They also confirm that actors, at whatever level, are never so rigidly constrained or hemmed in that progressive interventions are impossible.

That said, conflict is inherently part of the politics of progressive management, and can be expected to find an outlet in everyday encounters. Given the range of experiences and reactions discernible to date, people remain to be convinced, and are more likely to question or challenge innovations than commit themselves wholeheartedly on the assumption that subsequent initiatives will mark an improvement in their situation. Even the best of intentions will encounter opposition, although there is no reason to regard it as absolute or decisive. There is an abundance of evidence to demonstrate the folly of bracketing workplace opinion rigidly, or assigning people to hard and fast categories of outlook and behaviour (McCabe, 2000; Martin and Fryer, 1975).

This lesson became obvious with reactions to Fordism, although the workers who confront such an approach are still considered to exhibit an instrumental orientation to work. There is a continuing belief that manual workers are preoccupied with making money for a quality of life that is judged by factors beyond the workplace itself. In fact, this is frequently cited as a reason for not empowering staff, that the beneficiaries will not appreciate the efforts taken on their behalf, or will squander the opportunities. This line is rehearsed regularly in MBA classes and during research interviews (Hagen *et al.*, 2003), usually with the pronouncements of insensitive managers who assert that their own staff don't want it, or will not respond to it, because they take a calculating attitude to their work.

While the expression 'we're only in it for the money' can regularly be heard from workers, there is evidence that it does not represent a full or decisive view, or provide a reliable guide to behaviour. It is, in some cases, a defence mechanism, an internalised way of dealing with regimes that treat them as little more than 'pairs of hands' with no worthwhile brains to support a creative contribution. Consequently, people can warm to initiatives when they feel it safe to take them seriously. Just as Goldthorpe and Lockwood's

(1968) Vauxhall workers dramatically exploded the myths about their apathy and instrumentalism by taking strike action, so grassroots caution about work reform has occasionally given way to significant contributions by thoughtful and energetic people who can believe that there are genuine opportunities to make a difference (Blackburn, 1967; Beirne *et al.*, 1998a).

The struggles involved in developing this positive view of empowerment can be intense, however, generating frustration and calling for resilience and coping activities as much as an enlightened sense of engagement. Even the best of intentions can be tested by felt difficulties in dealing with contrasting views and challenging activities on a daily basis. The hassle factor can take a serious toll on committed actors, managers as well as employees, wearing them down and threatening their contribution.

Certainly, there have been casualties among forward-thinking managers. Talent has been lost to organisations that begin to experiment with empowerment, and to the broader movement for emancipatory management. Alan Pearson provides a notable example. He was the pioneering influence behind a broad range of team-based nursing initiatives within the NHS, including primary nursing (Beirne, 1999; Pearson, 1988). Sectional disputes and traditional decision-making prerogatives produced a level of disappointment and frustration that made it easier for him to take his insights and abilities to Australia (Channel 4, 1993).

There are also powerful examples of local managers who feel intimidated or stifled to the extent that they restrict their input, abandon enabling activities, and even make career choices that allow them to escape from uncomfortable pressures. A recent case comes to mind, where a junior manager at a utility company was called to account by his immediate superiors after encouraging meter reading crews to manage their own time and client contacts, without the need to 'sign in' or observe conventional and time-consuming controls. He reported that two other managers, including 'a twenty-two stone bully', told him 'not to be so bloody stupid' and to 'stop rocking the boat'. At this point, the spark went out of him. His response was to retreat, to deal with the situation in a very personal way, holding on to the belief that he would still be working with the company 'when these dinosaurs are long gone'. In the meantime, he would simply tread water, avoiding the pain and discomfort of 'sticking his neck out'.

Other managers, notably young graduates, use their qualifications to find an escape from such unpalatable experiences, even trying to put some distance between their own situation and the dilemmas involved in sustaining a progressive approach. A well-qualified graduate from the University of Glasgow recently resigned from a management position that was sought, on principle, with a major co-operative. After some two years of setbacks and difficulties in trying to articulate an empowering practice against an entrenched bureaucracy and traditional though inhibiting arrangements, she followed a very different route, resigning to promote brands of alcohol around the pubs and clubs of Central Scotland. The hassle attached to the management position was just too much for her to take, despite a strong commitment to grassroots empowerment and the expressed principles of the organisation.

These unhappy accounts of life at the sharp end of potentially progressive management are just as compelling as employee reports about false starts, constraints and disappointments. So what can be done to support those with a positive outlook, to develop their capacity for principled action and their resilience under fire?

CRITICAL COMMENTARIES AND PROGRESSIVE IMAGES OF MANAGEMENT

Critical thinkers have produced a rich library of insights and empirical evidence that has applied relevance as a means of cultivating analytical and interpretive capabilities. As noted at the outset, and laboured through previous chapters, critical research can sharpen local knowledge and personal experience by adding measured and discriminating insights into the problematics of empowerment. It provides enthusiasts with the chance to cultivate a broad appreciation of the dynamic issues tied into empowerment and direct participation, magnifying difficulties and constraints and highlighting the tensions and imbalances that affect practical initiatives.

Post-mortem studies and accounts of schemes that have faltered or backfired are especially useful, marshalling evidence that can help practitioners to anticipate contradictory tendencies, acknowledge contrasting interests, appreciate genuine concerns and attend to the sort of inconsistencies that were belatedly recognised at Volvo and elsewhere (Berggren, 1995; Beirne, 1999; Foster and Hoggett, 1999). Since management is a subject that is frequently reduced to technology and technique by n-step prescriptions (Tracy, 1990) that attempt to remove values and reflective intelligence from the agenda (Collins, 2000), critical research provides a sensitising rather than a numbing experience, raising personal awareness about the tensions and ambiguities involved, while building confidence and opening the sense of 'space for difference' among those who acknowledge progressive ideals. Yet management is also about activism and achievement. Liberated thinking and considered reflection are insufficient in themselves to secure collectively valued outcomes or deliver what a particular population might consider to be meaningful empowerment.

As argued in the Foreword, critical commentators have been less than effective in speaking to the challenges that confront practitioners who identify with progressive ideals. Some are content to explain what they are against rather than what they favour, while others map out the characteristics of a critical approach (Alvesson and Willmott, 1992) or wrestle with the difficulties of cultivating an appreciation for it through management learning and cognitive development (Mingers, 2000; Currie and Knights, 2003; Hagen *et al.*, 2003). Those with the most developed sense of practical activism have been working in specialist areas such as computing innovation, following the top-down approach of the driven theorist-practitioners identified in Chapter 3. For all the benefits that can be gleaned from this range of activity, there is a general need to attend directly to the practicalities of progressive management, to fill out the details of what it means to be critical and reflective, and to follow the logic of empowerment from the bottom up, giving everyday meaning to principled engagement.

This is where the traditions and conventions of collective art-making and community theatre may prove to be helpful. Historically, the visual and performing arts have made a significant contribution to critical management studies. There is a long and distinguished tradition of artists portraying the frustrations and harsh realities of working life, and prompting critical scrutiny of difficult or oppressive management regimes. Diego Rivera's murals depicting work under Fordism and the renowned Frank McGuinness play, *The Factory Girls*, provide notable examples. There are also important parallels in the way that artists have challenged prescriptive management thinking and the influence of consultancy advice within their own organisations.

Artists and arts workers are now active members of the broad-ranging community that passionately objects to the influence of over-rationalised conceptions of management (Protherough and Pick, 2002). Many of their organisations have passively imported 'expert solutions' from the corporate sector, unreflectively endorsing top-down controls and narrow job boundaries with little sense of counterproductive consequences (Beirne and Knight, 2002a). The strings attached to arts funding have put a premium on demonstrably 'sound' management and the effective use of resources. Consultants have been hired and familiar prescriptions traded and visibly applied, delivering work specialisation, promoting hierarchical control and putting a tight rein on resources, including staff. While satisfying the particular interests of funding agencies and showing a readiness 'to take management seriously', these developments have also had a damaging effect (Beirne and Knight, 2002a). Arguably the most significant, given prevailing levels of remuneration, is that the voluntary commitment that so many arts workers bring to their employment has been stifled, leaving them less inclined to be responsive to emerging needs or to work flexibly for positive results through their love of the art.

With the deliver-and-depart format of limited-budget management consulting, artistic directors and arts managers have been left to deal with the fallout from these episodes, including staff turnover, and are now among the most strident critics of rationalism (Beirne and Knight, 2002a; Protherough and Pick, 2002). Indeed, their sense of annoyance has been heightened by the predatory nature of consultants who peddle universal prescriptions with little sensitivity to the distinctiveness of arts organisations while at the same time appropriating art, reducing classical drama and theatre conventions to quirky motivational techniques and team-building exercises, for example (Moshavi, 2001; Clark and Mangham, 2004).

Rejecting such rationalistic impulses, critical commentators in the arts have argued for a more liberating conception of the relationship between art and management. Community theatre practitioners are among the most vocal and persuasive, drawing a distinction between imported techniques and the management practices that are applied to produce art in their own area. Their contention is that arts organisations should draw managerial value more directly from their own traditions and creative practices. However, this case has wider applicability. Established community arts practices have significant potential, not only as a means of counteracting unreflective managerialism, but also as a stimulus to creative thinking about the practical activism of emancipatory management.

There is a fundamental correspondence between critical reactions to rationalism in community arts and the transformative movements that have their roots in engineering and technological innovation (Bjerknes *et al.*, 1987; Greenbaum and Kyng, 1991) and in the critiques of management orthodoxy in the social sciences (including Alvesson and Willmott, 1992). They strike at rationalism from a common standpoint, rehearsing consistent themes and with dovetailing ideals that privilege active participation, reflective practice and negotiated learning (Beirne and Knight, 2002b). They stand for self-advocacy, ownership and equal access, favouring conditions that will enable people to develop their talent and realize their full potential. They are against authoritarianism, oppressiveness and hierarchical control, challenging the entrenched ideology that people are resources or commodities that function effectively when their opportunities for exercising discretion are restricted. Bringing their critical selves to the analysis of management, these commentators share a distaste for formats that privilege elite interests, highlighting problems of under-representation and taking silence in decision-making seriously as a cost, as a source of psychological, social, cultural and economic disadvantage.

Hence, community theatre, and more generally community arts, projects have largely developed in opposition to agency-led artistic programmes, certainly in Scotland where the latter have been criticised as patronising forms of artistic social work (see Herbert, 2004). The issue here centres on respect, for the participants as art-makers rather than for art as a civilising influence on 'subjects' that can be developed or improved by exposure to it. From this angle, the artistic process is bound up with the challenge of enabling ordinary people to take control of their lives and to play a part in shaping their world, not only in terms of culture, but socially and economically.

During the 1960s and 1970s in Scotland, the community arts were radicalised as forms of political articulation, education and debate. 'Cultural democratisation' became a rallying cry, not just for access to the arts but for socio-political activism and economic regeneration. The impetus came from the housing schemes of Edinburgh, Glasgow and Dundee where locally produced art was a catalyst for community development. It combined cultural expression with self-determination, mobilising working class and other disadvantaged groups to present arguments for improving their situations or surroundings through art that was capable of 'touching' politicians and decision-makers (Crummy, 1992; Herbert, 2004). Here is a process of engagement that brings people out of themselves, building confidence, releasing talent and creative energy while fostering collaboration and respect for 'otherness'.

In terms of principles and driving logic, this movement is entirely consistent with critical management studies. What it adds, however, is a more developed sense of alternative practice. Community artists are reaching beyond the critique of rationalism to reflect upon their own role as managers, capturing, formalising and generalising information about the effective running of collective arts projects. Their introspection and efforts to draw management insights from their own traditions of reflective practice provide a means of connecting critical thinking with everyday management activities, and of anticipating a qualitatively different approach that is empowering, accountable and principled.

CONNECTING ART WITH MANAGEMENT

Community artists aim to liberate artistic talent in local settings, to find creative ways of enabling people to make their own art. As previously indicated, their purpose is not to cultivate an appreciation for art that already exists, or to adopt a missionary role in delivering art to neighbourhoods that lack culture. Nor do they attempt to fit people into approved systems that ostensibly generate quality-assured art for local consumption. The point is that participants themselves become artists, that members of the public figure in the creative process of, say, producing involving drama or engaging in theatre that speaks to social concerns or connects with local issues. Creativity in this area is not confined to the 'inner world' of actors and artistic directors. It is not dependent on purveyors of independent expertise. Success requires the effective engagement of ordinary people, which means that the process must have relevance and authenticity. It needs to be grounded in the views, emotions and collective experience of the participants. The process is therefore relational, and the challenge of organising it ensures that management activities form an essential part of collective art-making.

Effective community artists are also de facto managers, co-ordinating and enabling participants to articulate their own values and express their views in a telling and effective manner. However, in this realm of the arts, very little can be achieved with a 'manager knows best' mentality. Successful outcomes depend on the artist's ability to move and motivate participants, to harness their talent and energy, and to promote shared learning and collective working. Active participation, critical reflection and negotiated learning are crucial managerial capabilities.

So what does this mean in practice? These artists often work with groups of people that are disadvantaged, vulnerable or troubled in some way. Progress is conditional upon nurturing and supporting their input, drawing them out of themselves, appreciating worries and concerns, and establishing the social ties that can support collaboration. By contrast with managerial preoccupations in work situations where the role of employees is often taken for granted, the participants in these empowerment schemes are the key reference points, the central focus of attention. Management only has meaning as a contextualised process of local learning and negotiated exchange as the arts practitioner endeavours to reach the participants, to appreciate their knowledge and experience, and respect their often unarticulated ability to perform in powerful or beautiful drama. This means finding the words, gestures and patterns of interaction that make their own contributions sincere and convincing. It means devising and developing collaborative arrangements as the work unfolds, continuously negotiating, reviewing and revisiting the terms of engagement with and between the participants. Management is therefore reconstituted as a sensitive, situated and relational activity that has nothing whatsoever to do with the transmission of abstract or universal expertise.

When interviewed about their practice, community artists often refer to the 'wealth' concept of negotiated learning as an underlying principle (Beirne and Knight, 2002a, 2004). This, again, puts the participants centre stage, acknowledging that people are generally capable, sensible and insightful, and therefore have a right to make decisions for themselves. The wealth conceptualisation puts the onus on the artist-as-manager to help participants collectively discover their best route to expression, and to provide them with 'an uncensored space' for artistic development. As one theatre practitioner recently explained:

> Each time we meet, we discuss our thinking and our reflections about the work...We are constantly trying to find the best way to make the story work. We endeavour to make sure that everyone's contribution is valued and heard as clearly as everyone else's (cited in Beirne and Knight, 2004, p. 38).

This model of engagement aims to uphold the dignity of the participants by creating safe structures and viable conditions for fruitful collaboration. These are purposefully created through active reflection and from a grounded understanding of the real-life concerns of the contributors and the dynamics of the situation. To quote one of the aphorisms of community theatre, 'the context is half the work'.

A recently published example should help to put this approach in perspective, to indicate the repertoire of ideas and possibilities that it encapsulates, and to establish its practicality beyond the many vague and unhelpful references to coaching and facilitating that characterise the empowerment literature (Beirne and Knight, 2004). Over a fifteen-month period, the Tuesday Afternoon Women's Theatre Group met in Edinburgh to devise and deliver a performance that celebrated their collective resilience and ability to struggle through life. The participants were all survivors of incest and sexual abuse, and were dealing with a very precarious, fragile and vulnerable existence. Their lives were shaped by risk and by the irregularities of being homeless, needing to hide and to avoid predictable patterns of living. Yet they had developed an interest in drama, having been encouraged to take part in a community arts programme, and were pushing for a project that would keep them involved. Their situations made it difficult to guarantee any sort of full and continuous collaboration, and there was always a danger of people falling out of the process for lengthy periods of time as other events took over their lives. Nonetheless, there was serious interest and a strong feeling that the experience could be helpful, so a team of community theatre practitioners developed a positive response.

As managers, their first task was to support the participants, to sustain their interest while keeping them secure and focused on activities that could deliver their ambition, to perform their own work in front of a live audience. This was a delicate challenge, encouraging the women to share their knowledge, to release insights and express views that had been forged through very painful experiences. Empowerment was conditional upon managerial sensitivity and reflective engagement. It required the artists-as-managers to read, interpret and respond to situations as events unfolded, and to reflect almost continuously upon the impact that their own activities had on others.

The initial priority was to find practical ways of establishing a safe working environment. Considerable effort was invested in building trust, and convincing the participants that they were not regarded as 'victims' by the artists or theatre crew. They were young women interested in making theatre, a message that was heavily reinforced with clear statements, regularly voiced, and with careful briefings for technical staff as they joined the production *en route* to performance. Other management tools were devised to establish an explicit consensus on the aims of the project and to cement working ties and relationships.

Early attention was given to a learning contract, and to openly negotiating its contents. Collective agreements and formal understandings of this nature figure prominently in community arts projects, synthesizing principles with ground rules and written standards of acceptable behaviour that increase the likelihood of productive collaboration. In this case, it was a flip chart list of points summarising why they were coming together, where they wanted to go, what they wanted to achieve, and how they would go about it. Given the sensitivities here, the emphasis was firmly on nurturing, sharing and supporting aspects, specifying landmarks and achievements that were to be celebrated along the way, and agreeing what people should do when they needed time out or a release from project work, for example. The list also included statements to reassure individuals that there was space for their input: 'everybody's contribution is valued'; 'everybody's ideas will be heard'.

Participants who had missed sessions or experienced difficulties with the process were brought back into the project by means of a drama exercise that gave them 'valuable gifts for reflection' from every other participant. These were offered from an imaginary basket of options, and would either emphasise the qualities they brought to the group or reveal hints and tips that would enable them to catch up with the others. Conversation would follow, with the core group talking through the latest deliberations and, significantly, explaining how the collective had held on to the individual's contribution since the last time they were together.

This case offers powerful and very practical examples of how mutual learning about people and situations can be combined with reflective thinking and a capacity for innovation to produce an enabling approach to management and organisation. These managers are breathing life into the alternative agenda, finding creative ways of engaging with people so that empowerment has meaning, so that participants can believe that their values and interests are shaping events, without the stifling interference of elitist, hierarchical or other debilitating influences.

The achievements of the women reached far beyond the hopes and expectations of anyone involved, including the survivors themselves. Their own accounts are quite candid in acknowledging the achievements of the artists-as-managers in nurturing their interests and enabling them to express hidden talents with positive results (Beirne and Knight, 2004). Keeping in touch with the situation proved crucial, investing the time and energy to develop an informed understanding and establish mutual respect, rather than assuming the mantle of aloof experts. This allowed the managers to recognise and accen uate key moments in the process and to add momentum.

About five months into the project, one young woman, who was having a particularly tough time coping with the attention of pursuers and official agencies, including the police, told the group how she had uncovered information about street children in Brazil. She explained that she would love to be able to teach them to survive as she had. The compassion she displayed during her own time of distress was transformational for the group. Recognising a turning point, the managers went into overdrive, searching for relevant images and stories, improvising ideas, and prompting the group to devise scenarios and develop characters. A consensus had emerged about the story line. Survival was now regarded as something to be celebrated.

Other theatre professionals were increasingly called into the process, although their introduction was carefully managed so that they could blend in without disrupting the flow. Most were women, including a costume designer, stage manager and scenic artist. Alex, the lighting man, was the most obvious exception, and he came to be trusted as 'a woman with a beard'. As the various parts of the project came together, the participants finally realized their ambition, performing their work for an audience drawn from their own communities, and including other survivors' groups. By all accounts, it was a moving and emotional occasion, attracting fulsome praise and admiration for the strength, resilience and creative achievements of the group (Beirne and Knight, 2004).

Again, the survivor's story offers a valuable insight into the practicalities and advantages of critical reflection and progressive management. It accentuates the nurturing and developmental role of management, although community theatre also casts light on less palatable, though equally important, aspects of alternative practice. There are other dilemmas and sources of unease in empowerment, such as whether and to what extent forceful and restricting activity is permissible.

This is not to be confused with a defence of managerial prerogatives, an endorsement of positional authority or a justification for commanding and controlling manoeuvres. It is a matter of counteracting factors that threaten, destabilise or otherwise undermine empowerment schemes, of containing divisive and disruptive influences, and of intervening to sustaining open and effective collaboration. Of course, this raises very thorny questions about compromise, slippage and even contradiction that utopian discussions avoid (for example, Hirschheim and Klein, 1994) yet practitioners confront on a regular basis. Threats to the integrity of empowerment arise not just from hierarchy, rationalism or traditional management preoccupations. They filter through from other sources of elitism and narrowly constituted sectionalism that challenge progressive managers, creating dilemmas of conscience and choice as they try to balance directly supportive activities with more forceful and restricting interventions.

In community arts, the problems posed by disruptive influences can be very obvious, especially in youth theatre and with drama projects for young offenders where the challenges and the possibilities for sustaining principled engagement have been tested for some time (Giesekam and Knight, 2000). Horseplay and chauvinistic posturing regularly command attention here, along with more disturbing examples of intimidating, distancing and vulgar behaviour. Clashing egos and sensitivities can inhibit collaboration, producing tensions and flashpoints that require careful handling. Contrasting interpretations about what it means to participate in drama, and what sort of engagement enhances or detracts from personal standing and credibility, can generate conflict among participants, or create an atmosphere in which some are hesitant, uneasy or fearful of ridicule and abuse.

By contrast with the survivor's case, collaborative working under these conditions requires a level of self-restraint and respect for others that does not always come easily to those involved. It also presents the arts practitioner with an immensely difficult situation to manage, in which to build supportive group ties, cultivate talent and secure positive outcomes from genuine collaboration. In this context, the responsibilities attached to empowerment, as well as the rights and opportunities, come sharply into focus. Success can depend on the artist-as-manager encouraging people to accept in others certain qualities or viewpoints that are not initially valued or even tolerated. It can be a matter of holding up a mirror to the outlook, orientation and even prejudice that participants bring to the activity, protecting some while connecting them to others.

While writers who express a Foucauldian allegiance may interpret this as providing approval for the reconstitution of subjects, for the shaping of identity so that people become more passive, compliant and willing (see Beirne *et al.*, 2004, for a discussion of this tendency), it is a basic and practical matter of struggling to engender dialogue and active collaboration. Again, the logic is to create safe structures, to establish uncensored space for negotiated learning and development, and to do so by tackling sources of oppression and suppression that lie beyond management orthodoxy. There are dilemmas and dangers in this, as indicated above. However, the issues are real and pressing for those at the sharp end of principled management, where mutual respect and open collaboration are problematic objectives rather than given qualities. In any case, as previous chapters have argued, there is no reason to believe that social actors are so easily manipulated or purged of their priorities, values and reflective capabilities.

Health and safety provides an obvious management issue where intervention on behalf of employees or project participants, that forcibly disrupts autonomous working in the interests of collective welfare, is legitimate. Whatever the level of sophistication or maturity achieved with empowerment, positive action to evacuate a burning building or disable dangerous equipment is as much of a priority for principled management as grassroots decision-making. Under these circumstances, forceful intervention can be liberating rather than threatening, assuming, of course, that it is based on accurate information about the physical dangers and viable escape routes.

Since it encapsulates a basic principle of engagement, this logic of intervention or interruption applies as much to internal as to externally generated threats, and to emotional as well as physical safety. The corollary is that management as principled activism involves manoeuvring and politicking, partly to inspire and enthuse, though also to structure the processes of exchange and engagement by acting against impediments, including those that emanate from the participant community itself.

During a recent young offenders project in Edinburgh, community artists used a variation of the learning contract mentioned earlier to challenge disruptive behaviour that was apparent from the outset, and to prevent it from getting out of hand. The flip chart agreement eventually became a typed document that was copied and distributed to all participants, reinforcing the message that 'violent behaviour will not be tolerated' and that there would be 'no fisticuffs or slagging off in workshops'.

This may be an extreme situation in management terms, yet it highlights the importance of imaginative responsibility, of developing inventive ways of shaping reciprocal exchanges to knit people together. This means acknowledging differences and tensions, and even asymmetrical qualities and forms of expression. Moreover, it means tackling them so that people are encouraged to expand their outlook, to relate personal development to collective engagement, and collaborate within a free and open discourse.

Mobilising for safe structures, or at least acting to reduce feelings of vulnerability, will, in some situations, involve painful management interventions to marginalize or outmanoeuvre interests that are incommensurable yet find expression in ways that threaten the collective endeavour. Where efforts to apply non-elitist values and establish terms of fair engagement are seriously undermined, say by violent or oppressive sectionalism, or by the restoration of Fordist controlling tendencies, the principles of managing for empowerment become entangled with the practicalities of defending the group.

Clearly, for community artists, empowerment is not a licence for participants to create chaos, so balancing liberating activities with restricting, curtailing and even removing interventions is an essential element of reflective and creative practice. With the young offenders initiative, there was a mixture of subtle and very forceful manoeuvres to remove persistent images of guns and weaponry from the drama, and to disempower some individuals who intimidated others and exploited the process for personal aggrandisement. Critical reflection called for unpalatable, difficult and often charged forms of practice that were reconciled with, or at least evaluated against, broader principles and the negotiated priorities of the wider community. Under this lens, empowerment is purged of its mythical status as a straightforward practice and a condition in which everyone gains. Woolly references to coaching, facilitating and even democratic engagement become irrelevant, floating free from any practical sense of the dilemmas that confront principled managers, and from any meaningful understanding of empowerment as a potentially contradictory and struggle-suffused approach to collaborative working.

NO METHOD, NO GURU, NO ILLUSIONS

Through their approach to collective art-making, community artists offer a glimpse of the liberating and transformative potential of reflective management. What is attractive, and what they envisage, is an intimate connection between accomplished art and responsive, context-sensitive management. There are no recipes here, or prescriptions that free the artists-as-managers from self-conscious reflection about the values they bring to situations, and the qualities they release in others. It is this situated blending of principle and practice, this balancing of learning, thinking and creative acting, that has wider applicability as a means of enlarging our sense of what is possible in managing to manage.

For those committed to empowerment and innovation, there is inspiration here to bring the alternative agenda to life, to lift the critiques of rationalism and dominating elites away from the bookshelves and out of the academic networks, and into the everyday experience of practising managers and enthusiasts for change. Successful community artists are able to move well beyond the classroom endorsement that 'decency matters', some of them finding very practical expressions of personal and collective empowerment. To borrow some terminology from Nord and Jermier (1992), these artists are finding ways to increase the congruence between humanistic values and everyday job performance. In some respects, the issue is forced for them as projects would fail and participants move rapidly on if declared principles were not apparent in the work. Yet the means of aligning beliefs with situated learning and creative forms of engagement is instructive.

Thinking back to the local experiences and predicaments identified at the beginning of this chapter, many potential and actual managers are actively seeking the sort of congruence that these artists achieve. For this constituency of critical thinkers, reflective art-making holds the promise of viable insights, resources and practical pointers to innovative behaviour that may help them to 'keep the faith', and perhaps recognise more of themselves in their everyday managerial work. It offers a cautiously optimistic agenda that can help managers to challenge established arrangements and elite interests, and bring progressive ideas to life in their own situations. There is a practical demonstration here of the scope for action in difficult circumstances, of the possibilities for creative engagement and mutual learning, despite pressing constraints and opposing or difficult behaviour by others.

Not that this is a model for management training. Community theatre practitioners are relying on improvisation and patterns of creative engagement that have been learned in practice and by networking with colleagues and, crucially, participants under particular project conditions. They draw not on formulas and prescriptions but on repertoires of established knowledge and emerging insights that they apply, appraise and develop in the context of unique situations. This is what gives their work authenticity and wider significance. By consciously and regularly relating their activities to the situated experiences of the people involved, these artist-managers demonstrate both the importance of reflective, interpretive and creative abilities, and the scope for others to develop and apply them. In this respect, their contribution expands the meaning that can be attached to 'reflection in action'.

In a frequently cited account of personal and professional sense-making, Schon (1983) uses this term to demonstrate that managers are self-aware people who actively think about their situations and experiences. Watson (1994) expands on this with an image of managers having debates within themselves as they make sense of what is happening around them and endeavour to exert some control over events. From here, reflective practice is a matter of sectional influence and advantage, of coping and thriving under prevailing conditions rather than developing a critique or principled activism that might challenge the status quo. With community theatre, reflection is more obviously connected to principles and collective engagement, and to the critical evaluation of how unfolding events stack up against them.

When reviewing their approach, theatre practitioners have talked about layers of learning and engagement that straddle the emotional, intellectual, creative and critical dimensions of their work (Beirne and Knight, 2004). At one level, they aim to be innovative, to become purposeful creators rather than users of managerial knowledge, exploring, improvising and trying things out. Experiential knowledge and networked information is applied as they structure encounters intuitively with ideas and behaviour that realized performances elsewhere and in the past. At the same time, they are trying to be systematic about their analysis, to stand back and consider reactions and developments, evaluating how principles and practice are coming together and using creative intelligence to address contradictions or emerging difficulties.

The advantage, when it all comes together, is that management is enacted in a way that contributes to empowerment and to valuable outcomes while maintaining a critical, and even attractively subversive, sense of identity. At a time when being critical is fashionable in management studies, and when few writers and researchers adopt non-critical positions, these artists offer a grounded and very practical view of what it means to be critical. They are active, both in deconstructing conventional concepts and categories, and in exploring alternative possibilities. They find space to reject narrow views and to pose other options, thereby engendering a sense of activism and awareness that is missing from a great deal of critical commentary.

The artist-managers discussed in this chapter are not unusual in working with conscious, responsive, purposeful and thinking human beings, although the women survivors and young offenders possibly provide a more compelling demonstration of human sensitivities than most employees at work. Nonetheless, managers in other contexts confront similar daily challenges in trying to operationalise their principles, give meaning to empowerment and enable the people around them to develop their potential. The insights afforded by community theatre provide these principled actors with positive images, constructive reference points and a realistic sense of difficulties and dilemmas. During the darker moments, when frustration grows and the pressures mount, the image of these managers and their struggles to maintain a consistent approach may help others to feel that they have room for manoeuvre and scope to express progressive values through management activity.

6.   Public policy and regulatory initiatives

Although there are genuine opportunities to nurture progressive thinking, support creative engagement and promote meaningful empowerment, committed practitioners face an uphill struggle to secure lasting change, for many of the reasons already indicated. Preoccupations with hierarchy, authority and decision-making 'rights' continue to exert a potent influence in management circles. Many employers, especially in Britain, remain tied to low-cost, limited-innovation strategies that privilege outsourcing, regimentation and high-intensity working, aided and abetted, of course, by influential consultants who present a view of 'modernisation' that is at odds with progressive images of empowerment.

The argument that employees are unhappy with responsibility, prefer routine jobs and take an instrumental approach to work is still rehearsed with remarkable regularity, asserted almost by reflex as a stock response to pressures for innovation. Moreover, in cases where the logic and momentum for change become irresistible, the suspicion and covert manoeuvring of managerial opponents frequently acts as a drag chain, hampering progress and promoting a snap-back to more conventional arrangements as conditions alter. As much of the evidence reported in this book confirms, workplace reform often amounts to a short-term, unsustained exercise that disappoints rather than inspires participants, reinforcing instead of transforming established attitudes, and adding bitter experiences that complicate the empowerment project.

Clearly, against this background and in light of these priorities, leaving progressive innovation to the voluntary commitment of principled actors may be insufficient to deliver lasting or generalised gains. Not that this renders their engagement pointless or futile, of course. The previous chapter clearly established the value of a personal commitment. The point here is to assess the strength of available institutional support structures, to discover whether public policies, typically in the form of legislative or negotiated programmes, provide the necessary prerequisites for sustainable innovation. Contesting, negotiating and struggling at local level become that much easier for innovators if the broader framework in which they operate is conducive, if public policy acts as a catalyst for meaningful empowerment and provides a viable resource base to 'lift' practitioners, build their resilience, encourage tenacity and offer them better opportunities to 'make a difference'.

Fortunately, in Europe, workplace participation has figured on the political agenda for a large number of years, certainly since the 1970s, and at worst as a background feature of employment policies and employee relations. Some politicians and policy-makers have openly argued for state and supra-state sponsored programmes that are capable of promoting progressive innovation, and have kept their ideas alive in policy discussions even when other issues and ideologies have been in the ascendancy, when Conservative governments in 1980s Britain expressly rejected such an approach, for example.

Government sponsorship has been identified as a crucial conditioning influence by officials and lobbyists associated with various political, industrial, trade union and research institutions, especially in the Nordic countries and continental Europe, as subsequent sections will reveal. Some commentators argue more specifically for legislative backing, presenting this as an essential ingredient if local initiatives are to strike roots and flourish (e.g. Bluestone, 1995, for the United States and Strauss, 1998, more generally). Guest (1997, p. 351) expresses this position succinctly: 'In the absence of any legislative framework, we can hope but we cannot be optimistic that employers will pursue enlightened practices'.

For justification, these commentators point to the operating arrangements of firms under different legal and institutional structures, noting how some readily dismantle or bypass participation schemes when requirements are eased or where they seem to be more relaxed, in managing labour in Spain or Britain as opposed to Germany, for instance. From here, legislation is necessary to protect and encourage the advocates and practitioners of workplace reform, to create an environment in which they can maintain a strong voice, avail themselves of opportunities to innovate, and exert a progressive influence on the policies and regular activities of their organisations. So what have legal and political programmes delivered? How does public policy support empowerment and innovation? Have national and supra-national initiatives been effective in speaking to the ambitions of progressive thinkers, or is decisive action required to 'move' policy-makers and create an enabling framework?

NATIONAL INITIATIVES

The economic preoccupations of policy-makers have added impetus to empowerment and workplace innovation, with a number of countries encouraging forms of participation and reorganisation by law or exhortation, specifically as a means of boosting international competitiveness. In the

1970s, Western governments, as economic managers, were exercised by the damaging effects of employee disaffection under buoyant labour markets, and were variously inclined to act on the view that absenteeism, labour turnover and damaging industrial relations were attributable to Taylorist job designs. Swedish, Norwegian and German administrations were among the most confident and purposeful, funding and co-ordinating programmes that promised to tackle these problems at their source by reorganising work, improving working conditions, enlarging the content of jobs and adding opportunities for participative decision-making (Ennals and Gustavsen, 1999; Alasoini, 2003).

More recently, trade liberalisation and globalisation have introduced additional pressures, subjecting governments to new constraints and structural challenges that have stimulated concerns for creativity, innovation and enterprise as the most lucrative values that can be generated in Western economies. Knowledge-intensive growth is now a privileged political objective, the acknowledged key to economic regeneration and future prosperity in a wider world of low-cost, high-volume manufacturers and service providers. Counteracting the effects of traditional management thinking, 'quick-fix' cost saving and cheap, high-intensity working, is more of a political priority (Department of Trade and Industry, 1999). Policy-makers are again openly and quite deliberately considering the role that governments and publicly supported programmes can play in developing workforce skills, promoting workplace innovation and changing the way that companies compete on the global stage.

The scope and intensity of government activity varies substantially, however, reflecting different ideological positions, as well as pragmatic concerns for legitimacy and political standing. As previously indicated, the Scandinavian countries, along with Germany, have a much richer history of progressive framing and intervention, although there have been suggestions that this has slipped in recent years, and that regional authorities and institutions have taken the lead with 'enabling' arrangements, particularly in Sweden (Alasoini, 2003). Nonetheless, the belief that work involves more than a contractual agreement between employers and employees, that the state has an obligation to underwrite minimum standards of employment and cultivate collaboration, remains strong in these countries.

Ambitious multi-year development programmes were launched in Norway and Finland during the 1990s, moving them to the forefront of publicly sponsored innovation (Ennals and Gustavsen, 1999; Payne and Keep, 2005). This was also a decade in which the Irish government announced that it was making a similar long-term commitment to partnership and work reorganisation. In Britain and the United States, by comparison, public policy debates followed a different course, betraying the influence of deregulatory interests in earlier Thatcher and Regan administrations. Patterns of state support for empowerment and employee relations were informed by very different values, by concerns for individualism rather than collectivism that challenged notions of partnership involving trade unions and nurtured a suspicion that regulatory proposals in this area would contradict the removal of trade barriers and inhibit the growth of free markets. These preoccupations are hardly conducive to the construction of complementary legal and institutional structures, hence Britain and the United States lag significantly behind Ireland, Germany and the Scandinavian countries in terms of infrastructure and the policy framework in which supportive arrangements can be devised, debated and advanced.

Successive Conservative governments in Britain during the 1980s and 1990s sought to create a market-based employment relationship, defending the 'freedom' and decision-making prerogatives of employers, regardless of whether they favoured the 'low road', minimum cost and investment, approach to staffing and work organisation. These were matters for the private sector and market forces, not for governments, although intervention to bolster this particular version of empowerment was considered to be appropriate. Conservative government support for participation was confined to tax incentive legislation that granted relief on Inland Revenue-approved employee share ownership and profit-sharing schemes. While these forms of financial participation grew significantly (Millward *et al.*, 2000), policy-makers anticipated that this would be at the cost of collectivism and trade union-based partnership arrangements. The point was to promote individualism through material involvement as opposed to decision-making rights and responsibilities, giving employees a direct stake in the fortunes of the employing organisation, loosening the attachment to trade unions and demonstrating that benefits can be realised if managers are allowed to operate without 'interference'.

The election of New Labour governments from 1997 ostensibly marked and secured a change of direction, with British policy-makers finally expressing a commitment to workplace innovation and to enhancing the quality of working life (Department of Trade and Industry, 1999). They are now apparently in tune with the enabling approach articulated by their counterparts in Northern Europe, having symbolically signed up to the provisions of the European Social Charter and the Social Chapter of the Maastricht Treaty, for example, both of which encapsulate this logic (Ramsay, 1991). Yet some commentators point to an abundance of rhetoric over substance.

Payne and Keep (2005) argue that the Blair governments have not substantially altered the policy trajectory that was set by the Conservatives in the 1980s. Lobbying institutions such as the UK Work Organisation

Network (UKWON) seem to agree, complaining that their representations have made little impression on policy and practice (Cressey, 2003; Payne and Keep, 2005). Continuities can certainly be identified in the association of markets and globalisation with organisational restructuring and the changing nature of work. Surprisingly for Labour politicians, faith in the 'invisible hand' of competition seems to be a surrogate for purposeful intervention, the assumption that markets will push firms towards empowerment, to reduce hierarchies and cultivate knowledge-workers allowing them to avoid conflict with employers and upsetting the business community by challenging 'low road' preferences.

There is an alternative explanation, however. New Labour reticence may be interpreted as a matter of political conviction, rather than signalling a lack of it. Support for the representational empowerment of trade unions, and for the partnership role they fulfil in Northern Europe, has been distinctly muted. Strengthening the position of unions, or indeed removing the legal constraints that were imposed upon them in the 1980s, has not been a policy objective. Conversely, New Labour has been keen to court business approval and respect managerial prerogatives as a pragmatic part of its broader political strategy. The endorsement of progressive framing and workplace innovation therefore conceals a particular view of partnership that contrasts with the approach taken in other European countries. Unions are being kept at arm's length while government sustains the so-called 'voluntarist' system of industrial relations in Britain, effectively distancing itself from an interventionist agenda.

There was more of an appetite to force the issue with employers in previous Labour governments, especially in the 1970s when policy-makers were engaged in struggles to change the governance structures of British companies. Ministers in the Callaghan administration that held office until 1979 favoured legislation to extend participative management into central areas of decision-making, notably by adding worker directors to the boards of major companies. The election that brought them to power in 1974 was contested on a manifesto commitment to legislate for 'industrial democracy', the phrase that focused debate and magnified different opinions about work and organisation at that time (Coates and Topham, 1980).

Looking to the experience of neighbouring countries, particularly Sweden and West Germany, and actively pursuing the tripartite model of partnership (between unions, employers and the state), this Labour government established a Committee of Inquiry under Lord Bullock in 1975 to find practical ways of introducing worker directors. Controversy raged through the deliberations, splitting the committee along conventional lines as the 'two sides of industry', employers and unions, expressed very different views on the logic, structure and extent of board level participation, on whether there should be single or two-tier arrangements and a separation of policy from supervisory matters, for example.

One of the employer representatives resigned, while the remaining three presented a minority report conceding that employees could legitimately be granted a presence in the boardroom as part of a participation agreement, though rejecting imposition. The consensus among other committee members, trade unionists and independents, was that the legislative case had merit, however. Their majority report, delivered in January of 1977, rehearsed arguments that resonate with more familiar, contemporary claims for empowerment:

> During our inquiry...we found a widespread conviction, which we share, that the problem of Britain as an industrial nation is not a lack of native capacity in its working population so much as a failure to draw out their energies and skill to anything like their full potential (Report of the Committee of Enquiry on Industrial Democracy, 1977, p. 160).

Although greeted with consternation in management circles, a watered-down version of the majority report's recommendations was translated into legislative proposals through a White Paper published in May 1978. The government was apparently keen to appease some of the critics and take a responsive approach to partnership, yet it was also flexing its muscles, demonstrating a willingness to intervene and to secure workplace innovation with an explicit regulatory framework. An election defeat in 1979 marked the end of this particular initiative, deflecting attention away from its relative strengths and weaknesses, since the incoming Conservative government, the first under Margaret Thatcher's premiership, had no intention of enacting legislation in this area, and was actually moving away from notions of partnership involving unions. The contrasts between the Labour administrations of Callaghan and Blair remain instructive, however, especially as they relate to contemporary developments in the countries noted for government intervention. As New Labour begins a third term in office, there is no sign of an equivalent stand on employee empowerment or workplace reform. Nor, as mentioned above, is there the same commitment to trade union channels of representation.

Arguably, this reflects a more sceptical turn in popular thinking about trade unionism, which on matters of work organisation and direct participation may indeed be warranted. Union movements in the Scandinavian countries have a much better record of mobilising, through partnership arrangements, to secure changes in the nature of work, and have rallied behind Quality of Working Life principles and initiatives, as illustrated in Chapters 2 and 3. Historically, British trade unions have shown very little interest in driving or shaping job reform schemes, confining their efforts to collective bargaining over wages and entitlements in employment.

This is not to say that strong unions with determined shop stewards and well-supported local organisations have been unable to influence job content and the introduction of work technology, or set constraints on managerial authority. There are examples of steward involvement in productivity agreements and of national officials (especially those representing clerical and white-collar workers) taking an interest in redesign episodes, with positive results arising from this in terms of work rate, environment and health and safety, for example (Flanders, 1964; Kelly, 1985). It would be stretching credibility, however, to equate this with a challenge to Taylorist orthodoxy, or as anything more than reactive and opportunistic bargaining.

Although union activity undoubtedly limited the diffusion of Taylorism in Britain during the early decades of the twentieth century, officials and negotiators have traditionally accepted and worked within its terms of reference, conceding managerial prerogatives and deferring to line management specialists on matters of work organisation (Littler, 1982; Loveridge, 1980). Hierarchy, job fragmentation and the principles of Taylorism and Fordism have generally been taken for granted, providing a context instead of a target for union activism. At the core of this lies a fundamental belief about the role and responsibilities of trade unions.

Officials, activists and many commentators in Britain, tend towards the view that unions are opponents, not of authoritarianism, rationalism or unitary conceptions, but of management *per se*. They endorse an adversarial system of industrial relations, lumping managers and trade unionists into clear-cut categories of allegiance, regardless of any values, orientations or dispositions that cut across the divide between employers and employees on the one hand, and their respective agents, managers and union officials, on the other. This perpetuates a reactive form of unionism that turns away from joint responsibility and shared decision-making, undercutting collaborative notions of partnership and casting unions as the 'opposition that can never become a government' (Clegg, 1960). By this account, independence is the key to effective representation, and the logic of trade unionism is to defend ground and bargain advantages from whatever management initiative comes along, be it Taylorism or participative job redesign. Accepting elements of management and sharing responsibility for the running of organisations increases the risks of incorporation, of unions assimilating management values and compromising their ability to secure the best deal for their members. As Clegg (1960) contends in the clearest statement of this position, participation has the potential to weaken unions, creating role confusion and neutralising their capacity to mobilise in support of an alternative agenda.

This fear was evident in reactions to the majority report of the Bullock Committee, when moderate and radical unions joined forces to oppose the case for worker directors with a level of hostility that matched some on the employer side. The Annual Reports of the Trades Union Congress reveal sharp exchanges and wrecking amendments as member unions tried to block any collective commitment to the majority report or expression of support for Bullock recommendations, asserting that the primary purpose of trade unionism is to oppose and to bargain. Again their fear was that negotiating positions would be undermined if worker directors were party to decisions that later became the focus of collective bargaining.

A variation on this oppositional view can also be detected in more recent critiques of the partnership arrangements developed within the European Union. Hyman (2005) argues that European integration is an elitist project that privileges economic interests while cheapening labour, creating unemployment and eroding social protection. By responding to overtures from the European Commission and accepting a role in regulatory projects, albeit to add a 'social dimension' to economic liberalisation, unions are ostensibly acquiescing to principles and forms of governance that damage the interests of their members.

For Hyman, the achievements of the union movement are founded on contention. Historically, they have secured benefits and protection for their members by challenging the prevailing social and economic orthodoxy, and mobilising support for an alternative agenda. His concern is that this capacity to contradict elite interests has been eroded by the institutionalisation of their relationships with employers, governments and more recently the European Union. Pragmatic and defensive interests have given impetus to partnership at the expense of contention, privileging formal and legalistic ways of maintaining legitimacy and influence against a background of industrial restructuring, recruitment difficulties and legislative restrictions from the Thatcher era. Though perhaps understandable, these survival instincts pose dangers for unions, according to Hyman, the pressure from an 'elitist embrace' (p. 24) weakening membership ties and the claims to moral legitimacy that were founded on contention.

Significantly, this opposition is connected to progressive struggling in Hyman's conceptualisation. He is appealing for advocacy as much as contention, for unions to rediscover their radical roots, to recapture the 'sword of justice' and present an alternative, 'moral economy'. This has not been such an obvious feature of institutionalised collective bargaining, however. As the established format for oppositional trade unionism, this in itself has produced a tendency to oligarchy and union sovereignty (Michels, 1949; Loveridge, 1980), privileging procedural regularity, and through this survival, while discouraging principled action either *against* Taylorism or *for* direct participation. Institutionalised contention, by this approach, is not self-evidently an ethical project. Nor does it signal the sort of progressive trade unionism that Hyman identifies with previous epochs. In fact, it exhibits contradictory tendencies, seeming to favour rather than counteract elitism by reproducing union channels of indirect representation and accepting authoritarian principles of work organisation at the expense of direct empowerment.

Oppositionalism has been less of a barrier in the Scandinavian countries where contention transparently ranges beyond ideology to practical matters of progress, outcomes and reform. Unions, employers and governments have repeatedly committed themselves to decentralised workplace developments and to jointly governed regulatory initiatives. There is a long history of dialogue and collaboration in Norway, Sweden and Finland that has given meaning and purpose to tripartite notions of partnership, focusing policy and practice and adding impetus to innovation. Rather than simply contributing to discussions, representatives of employers' organisations and union confederations have worked alongside government officials, initiating, co-ordinating and managing development programmes, as well as sharing in some of the funding (Gustavsen *et al.*, 1996; Alasoini, 2003; Payne and Keep, 2005).

Although activity levels have fluctuated with national political trends and economic conditions, this framework has reinforced the legitimacy of workplace reform while establishing conducive conditions for successive waves of innovation, from the Norwegian Industrial Democracy programme of the 1960s and 1970s, through humanistic manufacturing and alternative technology movements in Sweden, and on to national innovation projects that connect empowerment and job restructuring to enterprise and organisational renewal (such as Enterprise Development 2000 and Value Creation 2010 in Norway). These programmes have captured international interest and approval, claiming space for partnership as a potentially viable arena in which to mobilise in favour of reform and against orthodoxy.

Studies of supported projects point to workplace gains in teamworking and co-operation within and across the traditional boundaries between employees, managers and specialists, leading to improvements in productivity, quality and flexibility (Alasoini, 2003; Payne and Keep, 2005). Though reliant on survey data and the recollections and impressions of key stakeholders, the available research offers a very positive assessment, with impressive approval ratings reported per category of respondent. Trade unionists have been a little more restrained than managerial and employee grades, yet a high proportion of those affected by publicly sponsored programmes across the various countries evidently take partnership to be a constructive rather than threatening development (Gustavsen *et al.*, 1996; Alasoini, 2003).

The effects on infrastructure and the broader environment in which activists operate are considered to be particularly significant. The Scandinavian programmes have traditionally given partnership roles to research institutes and social scientists as a means of expanding the boundaries on innovation, of posing fresh options and looking beyond existing assumptions and business preconceptions. Ideas and experiences have been shared as the relationships between the research and practitioner communities have developed, adding to the stock of available knowledge that innovators can call upon, creating interactive learning networks that foster dialogue and co-operation across wider communities, and building a 'critical mass' in favour of empowerment and innovation (Alasoini, 2003; Payne and Keep, 2005).

Not that progress is assured, even under these ostensibly propitious conditions. There have been setbacks and difficulties in capitalising upon the local achievements of the major national programmes, with evidence underlining concerns about diffusion and sustainability. Innovations within particular areas or facilities have failed to secure wider support, or trigger general changes across sectors or organisations (Alasoini, 2003; Qvale, 2002). Enthusiasts have confronted major problems in moving the wider population of employers and stakeholders beyond expressions of interest, and in translating awareness into broader-ranging capacities for action. Doubts have also been expressed about directed change, echoing earlier Swedish critiques of top-down approaches that contradict the logic of empowerment and risk employee disaffection, as indicated in Chapter 3 (Payne and Keep, 2005). For these reasons, judgements about the value of national programmes have been tempered with disappointment, and frustration at the continuing difficulty of agreeing terms and establishing criteria for consistent local initiatives. These persistent concerns apply to more than just national regulatory schemes, however.

THE ROLE OF THE EUROPEAN UNION

Arguably, the European Union provides the most significant regulatory stimulus to workplace reform, specifically through the social provisions that aim to protect citizens from the deleterious effects of unrestrained competition (Gill *et al.*, 1999; Gill and Krieger, 2000). Claims for wider employee participation have influenced the European social agenda since the beginning of the 1970s, with an influential community of policy-makers articulating a vision of participative management and corporate governance that is consistent with Quality of Working Life principles and sympathetic to trade union representation. Their efforts have been controversial, however, provoking heated debates and triggering political compromises that have restricted the scope of practical initiatives. As Hyman (2005) has observed, Europe is a contested territory, where the momentum behind economic integration has not been matched by a consensual politics of workplace development and organisational renewal. Reports about the impact of 'social Europe' in this direction tend to be highly qualified, and subject to regular expressions of frustration from enthusiasts for reform.

Yet, there have been some very ambitious attempts to structure empowerment and promote innovation at the European level. Reflecting the broad interest in industrial democracy during the 1970s, the European Commission sought to legislate for employee rights to formal representation on the governing bodies of public limited companies. The draft Fifth Directive, presented in October 1972, proposed a two-tier structure of supervisory and management boards, backed by statute, that would grant decision-making influence to the grassroots in undertakings with fifty or more staff. This was followed in 1980 by the Vredeling Directive, named after then Social Affairs Commissioner, Henk Vredeling, which sought greater levels of transparency around corporate affairs, with formal rights to information and consultation for employees of multinational companies.

These proposals sparked intense controversy, having little impact in the face of concerted opposition from business interests and lobby groups acting on behalf of many multinationals (Ramsay, 1991). European legislators were not moved to ratify them at the stage, although by the end of the 1980s policy-makers were more amenable to action on this front, anticipating the creation of a potent regulatory framework that was capable of advancing participation.

This renewal of interest, and even determination, was founded upon the realization that economic liberalisation and the arrival of the single European market would pose problems and generate tensions if the market-making mission was not counterbalanced by suitably sensitive social and employment policies. This sense was heightened by events within multinationals such as Hoover, where executives were setting plants against each other to force changes in working practices, threatening redundancies or actually concentrating operations in areas where employees were prepared to accept more 'flexible' jobs, 'no-strike agreements' and far-reaching changes in terms, conditions and their psychological contract. 'Social dumping' was a particular worry for politicians and trade unionists in Germany and France, where pressure mounted to counteract any flight of capital to countries that could offer cost advantages by reducing the social responsibilities and regulatory requirements on firms. The preference here was to 'level-up' in terms of standards and regulatory provisions, and to improve competitive performance across Europe with enhanced forms of work organisation, skill development and collaboration between the social partners, employers, employees and trade unions.

Out of this came the Social Charter and the idea of a basic platform of fundamental rights and protections that would complement emerging commercial opportunities, and generate employee consent for performance improvements by securing effective channels of influence. Workers' rights to life-long learning, vocational training, freedom of association and movement between jobs, health and safety protection, and an 'equitable' wage, sit alongside benefit entitlements to 'adequate' social security and income after retirement in a framework that was endorsed in December 1989, and reinforced by the Social Chapter of the 1993 Maastricht Treaty. Through this period, policy-makers at the centre of the European project were aiming to accelerate the passage of legislation that would deliver the rights enshrined in the Charter, clearing obstacles to the legislative package (the Social Action Programme, as it is formally designated) as part of a movement towards closer European Union.

At that stage, the blocking policy of successive British Conservative governments (that were steadfastly against 'Social Europe' on the grounds that it compromised trade liberalisation, the operation of the Single market and the restrictions that Thatcher administrations applied to British trade unionism) was targeted, and apparently bypassed, with a rule change that brought Qualified Majority Voting to employment matters, meaning that no single state could prevent the passage of a law to which it alone objected. This provoked intense debate about the impact of European regulation at the time, especially when then Prime Minister John Major claimed to have negotiated an exemption from the Social Chapter. Judgements about the significance or otherwise of this for British companies, managers and workers became redundant, however, when New Labour embraced the Social Chapter and Charter shortly after taking office in 1997.

With this development and seemingly wide consensus on regulation, the pan-European approach now promises meaningful progress. For some commentators, the Charter, Chapter and accompanying Action Programme represent the high-water mark of regulatory achievement (Gill *et al.*, 1999, p. 315). Extending workers' rights to information, consultation and participation over matters that directly affect their employment is central to the framework, and to the most significant achievement of the legislative programme so far. The aspirations that were invested in the Vredeling and draft Fifth Directives were given new form and focus with the European Works Councils Directive of 1994.

This requires the creation of a European Works Council (EWC) or, alternatively, some other agreed procedure for informing and consulting workers in every 'Community-scale' multinational company, defined as one with more than 1,000 employees within the European Union and at least 150 in each of two member states. With this Directive, European policy-makers finally established the legal foundations for a transnational approach to participative management, giving employee representatives information and consultation rights on organisational changes, investments, the introduction of new technologies, processes and working methods, production transfers and plant closures, mergers, cutbacks and redundancies. Estimates vary on the proliferation of EWCs since the Directive came into force (outside Britain) in September 1996, although reliable indicators point to a steady growth pattern, from approximately 550 by mid-1999 (Gill and Krieger, 2000) to around 700 in 2003 (Hall and Marginson, 2005; Cressey, 2003). This is from a projected total of 1,850 eligible companies prior to the latest enlargement of the Union in 2004, which brought an additional ten countries within the scope of the Directive (Hall and Marginson, 2005).

This expansion coincides with a discernible shift in European thinking about participation and regulation, possibly moderating its impact, however. Since the mid-1990s, policy pronouncements have favoured direct forms of participation and, perhaps more significantly, 'softer' methods of leadership and 'steering' over imposition by recourse to directives (Gill *et al.*, 1999; Hyman, 2005). This is evident in the European Commission's 1997 Green Paper *Partnership for a New Organisation of Work* and its 1998 communication, *Modernising the Organisation of Work: a positive approach to change.* Both rehearse familiar arguments about the association of workplace innovation with competitive success, extolling the virtues of upskilling, flexible working and the benefits to be gleaned from investing in local empowerment and direct participation. They call for new working relationships and meaningful departures from the traditional forms of hierarchy and specialisation that are rooted in adversarial Taylorism, though putting the onus firmly on managers to prioritise and drive change programmes at the level of the firm.

Of course, there is a recognition that many managers will struggle with this sort of adjustment, and that progress will be uneven and occasionally fraught. This has been weighed against employer suspicions of statutory intervention, however, and a history of dismissive and often hostile reactions to regulation through indirect participation involving unions and third party agencies (Gill and Krieger, 2000). The upshot is that European policy-makers are now accentuating the voluntary and negotiated aspects of change. There is a stronger emphasis on agreements that are in tune with local circumstances, and a vision of Europe as an arena populated by opinion formers, leaders and co-ordinators.

This is not to suggest that the European Commission has rejected regulation, or abandoned purposeful action for a relatively passive stance. The point is rather that legislative intervention is now predominantly regarded as a matter of last resort, as a fallback where voluntary agreements prove to be elusive. The latest vocabulary of European policy-making reflects this shift, with references to 'soft law' and 'social benchmarking' presented to cultivate a user-friendly image and counteract any worries that the social partners may have about enforcement or the imposition of a standard European regime.

The EWC Directive itself asserts the primacy of negotiations between the social partners. By contrast with the 1970s proposals, it makes a point of avoiding 'hard law' regulation, allowing representatives of employees and employers to specify the precise nature, composition, function and procedures of EWCs, and the financial resources necessary to sustain them. They can even decide that councils are inappropriate, so long as they reach agreement about alternative procedures for informing and consulting staff. It would only be after three years of stalemate or inactivity that the Directive's 'subsidiary requirements' would take effect, imposing the minimum standard of an EWC with between three and thirty members, fully representing the member states in which the company operates, meeting at least once a year to exchange information, or under the exceptional circumstances of plant closure, relocation or collective redundancies. Significantly, employee representatives on these councils have no rights to challenge managerial prerogatives or obstruct management decision-taking.

This 'soft touch' approach to innovation, together with the minimalist, 'pick and mix' flexibility of the EWC Directive, has attracted criticism from commentators and council members who detect some slippage from original principles and a shortfall in achievements relative to aspirations and declared intentions (Waddington, 2003; Cressey, 2003; Hyman, 2005). Although early reports from the Trades Union Congress and Labour Research Department were positive, especially about the forerunner voluntary EWCs (introduced prior to September, 1996) that were ostensibly fulfilling their role of informing and consulting (Gill *et al.*, 1999; Hall and Marginson, 2005), substantial grassroots benefits are difficult to detect. In fact, there is considerable dissatisfaction, and a growing sense that EWCs in practice amount to rather empty talking shops that pose difficulties for the future of empowerment rather than securing genuine influence.

With the leeway afforded to managers, it is difficult to be strongly optimistic that EWCs constitute a truly effective means of combating traditional constraints on empowerment. Surveys of managerial opinion suggest that a narrow view of their role and relevance predominates, that outright opposition is not necessarily the tactic that traditionalists pursue *against* EWCs, and that those who are inclined to defend managerial prerogatives have been able to bend them to their own advantage (Wills, 1999; Cressey, 2003). Wills (1999) discovered a tendency for EWCs in practice to strengthen hierarchical management, to be used as an additional means of corporate communication, and even to be absorbed within a culture management agenda as an extra conduit for promulgating official values across European operations. She also found that instead of accommodating or responding to input from employee representatives, some companies were using council arrangements to contain union influence, pitting trade unionists against non-union delegates or nominees for council seats.

This evidence is consistent with the findings from case study investigations conducted by Waddington (2003) and also by Marginson *et al.* (2004). These authors point to variations in the impact of EWCs between companies headquartered in Britain and the United States and those based in continental Europe. However, the overall effects are judged to be modest, the differences relating to the implementation of management decisions rather than their substance. The prevalence of a more restrictive approach among British and American nationals, even on these very contained terms, is largely attributed to Anglo-Saxon management traditions and the hold that essentially Taylorist values and preoccupations continue to have on practitioners. The case study councils tended to reflect and reproduce these aspects rather than challenge them, although the effects were moderated to some degree when arrangements were handled by European nationals and within the management structures of continental operations. Established traditions also had a bearing upon the perceptions of employee representatives, those from Anglo-Saxon companies registering lower levels of dissatisfaction than their continental, and especially Nordic, equivalents, partly because they were starting with weaker expectations founded upon previous experience. Nonetheless, the role of the councils, the scope for discussion and the information tabled were more obviously and heavily circumscribed in these cases, especially in multinationals headquartered in Britain.

Clearly, on this evidence, there is wide-ranging scope for management traditionalists to thrive within the European regulatory framework. Only a small minority of respondents associated EWCs with negotiated change and meaningful empowerment. This is not to say that limited outcomes are inevitable or that struggles are somehow neutralised within this arena. There are some encouraging reports of participative practice and substantive joint decision-making, of EWCs that reach beyond the limited rights enshrined in the Directive and hold their ground fairly well (Lecher *et al.*, 2001; Hall and Marginson, 2005). The agency of committed participants seems to have been critical in these cases, with employee representatives in particular given credit for imaginative practice, recognising new opportunities for networking and collective engagement on a wider scale. This marks the exception rather than the rule, however, with workforce representatives generally failing to 'punch their weight within EWCs', certainly in the case of British trade unionists (Hall and Marginson, 2005, p. 215).

That said, the representatives covered by Waddington's study (2003) broadly welcomed the principle of EWCs and European regulation. Their dissatisfaction with tactical management and limited information was channelled into calls for additional regulation, for a revision and general tightening of the Directive to deliver meaningful participation. This is patently a trade union position, however, which does not of necessity resonate with opinions on the shop floor. Social Europe undoubtedly appeals to trade unionists, promising a formal role through prevailing notions of partnership and indirect participation that may help them to consolidate their position and claim space for relevance in turbulent times (Hyman, 2005). Expressions of indifference or irrelevance are more likely at workforce level since EWCs have evidently not fulfilled a transformative role or secured general improvements in the daily experience of working life.

BEYOND 'SOFT LAW' POLITICS

Available opportunities to extend the scope of progressive management and enact a principled commitment to empowerment and workplace innovation are undoubtedly influenced by wider political movements that operate to structure organisational relations. Developmental issues have clearly captured attention and provided a focus for the mobilisation of resources within these, policy-makers demonstrating awareness, allied to variable capacities for action, at national and supranational levels.

Yet the existing regulatory architecture across the areas reviewed in this chapter is generally weak, and too easily compromised or ignored by those who either regard empowerment and participative management as inimical to their interests, or seek to bend and contain these concepts within tight boundaries. Of course, it would be crass to deny the sincerity of the politics behind these regulatory initiatives, or condemn them as empty gestures. Any tendency towards symbolic posturing has to be set against the determined struggles of the policy-makers who advanced the national workplace development programmes and European initiatives considered here, usually against significant opposition and rearguard politicking. Their efforts have taken the empowerment project forward, though mainly in a supportive, incremental and non-regulatory fashion, through exhortation and encouragement, by keeping the agenda alive for front-line enthusiasts, adding momentum to networking and coalition-building, and by fostering a climate that is conducive to the cross-fertilisation of ideas (Hall and Marginson, 2005; Payne and Keep, 2005; Alasoini, 2003, Hyman, 2005).

However, there is more to progress than positive statements and solemn declarations of the sort invested in the Social Charter, important as these are in contextualising innovation. Nor is it a matter of creating propitious conditions and outline structures, especially when these slip to minimalism in applied content, providing an outlet for token participation, reluctantly enforced when employers simply refuse to observe due process (for example, with EWCs). Supportive programmes need to make a difference at the grassroots, where practitioners confront constraints on a regular basis. In this respect, the regulatory initiatives developed in Britain, across Europe and even in the Scandinavian countries (according to the research reported in this book) have not been radical enough.

Front-line enthusiasts remain vulnerable and exposed, relying upon their own agency and collaborative ties, with insufficient protection from enlightened regulatory sources. Under these conditions, casualties of the sort described in Chapters 3 and 5 are likely to grow in number. This is the hard end of 'soft law' politics. If innovators are to flourish and advance empowerment rather than succumb to the pressures from orthodoxy, legal and institutional provisions need to be fixed at the centre of publicly sponsored programmes, not mildly or tentatively included as a backdrop to persuasion and dialogue. Considering the available evidence, it seems difficult to avoid the conclusion that regulatory interventions need to be more focused and much sharper. Of course, this intensifies the politics of empowerment and innovation, putting a premium on reflective abilities, capacity-building and determined struggling, in policy-making as much as management.

Bibliography

Ackers, P., Marchington, M., Wilkinson, A. and J. Goodman (1992), 'The use of cycles? Explaining employee involvement in the 1990s', *Industrial Relations Journal*, 23, pp. 268–283.

Adler, P. (1993), 'Time and motion regained', *Harvard Business Review*, January, pp. 97–108.

Adler, P. and R. Cole (1993), 'Designed for learning: a tale of two plants', *Sloan Management Review*, Spring, pp. 85–91.

Alasoini, T. (2003), 'Promotion of workplace innovation on the public policy agenda: reflections on the Finnish workplace development programme', UK Work Organisation Network, working paper number 5.

Alvesson, M. and H. Willmott (1992), (eds), *Critical Management Studies*, London: Sage.

Anthony, P.D. (1977) *The Conduct of Industrial Relations*, London: Institute of Personnel Management.

Anthony, P. (1994), *Managing Culture*, Buckingham: Open University Press.

Argyris, C. (1998), 'Empowerment: the emperor's new clothes', *Harvard Business Review*, 76, pp. 98–105.

Arkin, A. (1995), 'The bumpy road to devolution', *People Management*, 1, pp. 34–36.

Bachrach, P. and A. Botwinick (1992), *Power and Empowerment: a radical theory of participatory democracy*, Philadelphia: Temple University Press.

Baddon, L., Hunter, L., Hyman, L., Leopold, J. and H. Ramsay (1989), *People's Capitalism: a critical analysis of profit-sharing and employee share ownership*, London: Routledge.

Bansler, J. and K. Bodker (1993), 'A reappraisal of structured analysis: design in an organisational context', *Transactions on Information Systems*, 11 (2), pp. 165–93.

Barker, J. (1993), 'Tightening the iron cage: concertive conflict in self-managed teams', *Administrative Science Quarterly*, 38, pp. 408–437.

BBC (1994), 'The computer triangle, *The Money Programme*, BBC2, 16th January.

BBC (1995), 'Videoprint', *Sid's Heroes*, BBC1, 14th May, 11.30 a.m.

BBC (2000), 'Changing the Japanese Way', *Bubble Trouble*, BBC 2, January.

BBC (2002), 'Production methods', *Working Lunch Business Education*, BBCi, 31st January.

Beath, C. and W. Orlikowski (1994), 'The contradictory structure of systems development methodologies: deconstructing the IS-user relationship in information engineering', *Information Systems Research*, 5 (4), pp. 350–377.

Beirne, M. (1999), 'Managing to empower ? A healthy review of resources and constraints', *European Management Journal*, 17 (2), pp. 218–225.

Beirne, M. and S. Knight (2002a), 'Principles and consistent management in the arts: lessons from British theatre', *The International Journal of Cultural Policy*, 8 (1), pp. 75–89.

Beirne, M. and Knight, S. (2002b), 'Principles and the practice of reflective management', proceedings of the First International Art of Management and Organisation Conference, Kings College, London, September.

Beirne, M. and S. Knight (2004), 'The art of reflective management: dramatic insights from Scottish community theatre', *The International Journal of Arts Management*, 6 (2), pp. 33–43.

Beirne, M. and H. Ramsay (1988), 'Computer redesign and labour process theory: towards a critical appraisal', in Knights, D. and H. Willmott (eds), *New Technology and the Labour Process*, London: Macmillan, pp. 197–229.

Beirne, M. and H. Ramsay (1992), 'A creative offensive? Participative systems design and the question of control', in Beirne, M. and H. Ramsay (eds), *Information Technology and Workplace Democracy*, London: Routledge, pp. 92–120.

Beirne, M., Ramsay, H. and N. Panteli (1998a), 'Participating informally: opportunities and dilemmas in user-driven design', *Behaviour and Information Technology*, 17 (5), pp. 301–310.

Beirne, M., Ramsay, H. and N. Panteli (1998b), 'Developments in computing work: control and contradiction on the software labour process', in Thompson, P. and C. Warhurst (eds) *Workplaces of the Future*, London: Macmillan, pp. 142–162.

Beirne, M., Riach, K. and F. Wilson (2004), 'Controlling business? Agency and constraint in call centre working', *New Technology, Work and Employment*, 19 (2), pp. 96–109.

Berggren, C. (1992), *The Volvo Experience: alternatives to lean production in the Swedish auto industry*, Basingstoke: Macmillan.

Berggren, C. (1995), 'Are assembly lines just more efficient? Reflections on Volvo's "humanistic" manufacturing', in Babson, S. (ed.), *Lean Work: empowerment and exploitation in the global auto industry*, Detroit: Wayne State University Press, pp. 277–291.

Beynon, H. (1973), *Working for Ford*, London: Allen Lane.

Bjerknes, G., Ehn, P. and M. Kyng (1987), (eds), *Computers and Democracy: a Scandinavian challenge*, Avebury/Gower.

Blackburn, R. (1967), 'The unequal society', in Blackburn, R. and A. Cockburn (eds), *The Incompatibles: trade union militancy and the consensus*, Harmondsworth: Penguin, pp. 15–55.

Blomberg, J., Kensing, F. and E. Dykstra-Erickson (1996), 'PDC'96'. proceedings of the participatory design conference, Cambridge, Massachusetts 13th-15th November, Palo Alto: CPSR.

Bluestone, I. (1995), 'Public policy and the evolution of change in industrial relations', in Babson, S. (ed.) *Lean Work: empowerment and exploitation in the global auto industry*, Detroit: Wayne State University Press, pp. 350–361.

Blum, B. (1996), *Beyond Programming: to a new era of design*, New York: Oxford University Press.

Blumberg, P. (1968), *Industrial Democracy: the sociology of participation*, London: Constable.

Boguslaw, R. (1965), *The New Utopians: a study of system design and social change*, Englewood Cliffs, New Jersey: Prentice Hall.

Brannen, P., Batstone, E., Fatchett, D. and P. White (1976), *The Worker Directors: a sociology of participation*, London: Hutchinson.

Briefs, U., Ciborra, C. and L. Schneider (1983) (eds), *Systems Design, For, With and By the Users*, Amsterdam: North Holland.

Brown, R. (1984), 'BSA Presidential Address: working on work', *Sociology*, 18 (3), pp. 311–323.

Bruce, M. (1987), 'Managing people first: bringing the service concept into British Airways', *Industrial and Commercial Training*, March/April, pp. 21–26.

Buchanan, D. (2000), 'An eager and enduring embrace: the ongoing rediscovery of teamworking as a management idea', in Procter, S. and F. Mueller (eds), *Teamworking*, Basingstoke: Macmillan, pp. 25–42.

Buchanan, D. and D. Preston (1992), 'Life in a cell: supervision and teamwork in a manufacturing systems engineering environment', *Human Resource Management Journal*, 2 (4), pp. 55–76.

Burnes, B. (1998), 'Recipes for organisational effectiveness: mad, bad or just dangerous to know?', *Career Development International*, 3 (3), pp. 100–106.

Burns, P. and M. Doyle (1981), *Democracy at Work*, London: Pan Books.

Burns, T. (1967), 'Sociological explanation', *British Journal of Sociology*, 18 (4), pp. 353–369.

Caudron, S. (1995), 'Create an empowering environment', *Personnel Journal*, September, pp. 28–36.

Channel 4 (1993), *The Pulse*, series 1, programme 10, 5th May, London: Diverse Productions.

Ciulla, J. (2000), *The Working Life: the promise and betrayal of modern work*, New York: Random House.

Clark, T. and R. Fincham (2002) (eds), *Critical Consulting: new perspectives on the management advice industry*, Oxford: Blackwell.

Clark, T. and I. Mangham (2004), 'From dramaturgy to theatre as technology: the case of corporate theatre', *Journal of Management Studies*, 41 (1), pp. 37–59.

Clegg, H. (1960), *A New Approach to Industrial Democracy*, London: Blackwell.

Clement, A. (1993), 'Looking for the designers: transforming the invisible infrastructure of computerised office work', *AI and Society*, 7, pp. 323–344.

Clement, A. (1994), 'Computing at work: empowering action by low-level users', *Communications of the ACM*, 37 (1), pp. 53–63.

Coates, K. and T. Topham (1980), *Trade Unions in Britain*, Nottingham: Spokesman.

Collins, D. (1999), 'Born to fail? Empowerment, ambiguity and set overlap', *Personnel Review*, 28, pp. 208–221.

Collins, D. (2000), *Management Fads and Buzzwords: critical-practical perspectives*, London: Routledge.

Commission of the European Union (1998), *Modernising the Organisation of Work: a positive approach to change*, Luxembourg: Office for the Official Publications of the European Union.

Conti, R. and M. Warner (1993), 'Taylorism, new technology and just-in-time systems in Japanese manufacturing', *New Technology, Work and Employment*, 8 (1), pp. 31–42.

Cooley, M. (1980*), Architect or Bee?*, Slough: Langley Technical Services.

Cressey, P. (2003), 'European works councils – transforming European industrial relations?', *UK Work Organisation Network Journal*, 1.

Crummy, H. (1992), *Let the People Sing!*, Edinburgh: Craigmillar Festival Society.

Cunningham, I., Hyman, J. and C. Baldry (1996), 'Empowerment: the power to do what?', *Industrial Relations Journal*, 27, pp. 143–154.

Currie, G. and Knights, D. (2003), 'Reflecting on a critical pedagogy in MBA education', *Management Learning*, 34 (1), pp. 27–49.

Curtis, B., Krasner, H. and N. Iscoe (1988), 'A field study of the software design process for large systems', *Commnications of the ACM*, 31 (11), pp. 1268–1287.

Daily Record (1996), 'BA in shop-a-mate storm', 12th October, p. 9.

Daily Record (1998), 'Make fat cats pay', 23rd July, p. 8.

Daily Record (2003), 'Fatcats trouser 288% rise', 10th October, p. 2.

Danford, A. (1997), 'Teamworking and labour regulation: a case study of shop floor disempowerment', Proceedings of the 15th International Labour Process Conference, Edinburgh, March.

Danford, A., Richardson, M. and M. Upchurch (2003), *New Unions, New Workplaces: a study of union resilience in the restructured workplace*, London: Routledge.

Davis, L. and J. Taylor (1972) (eds), *The Design of Jobs*, Harmondsworth: Penguin.

Deal, T. and A. Kennedy (1982), *Corporate Cultures: the rites and rituals of corporate life*, Harmondsworth: Penguin.

Deal, T. and A. Kennedy (1999), *The New Corporate Cultures: revitalising the workplace after downsizing, mergers and reengineering*, Cambridge, Massachusetts: Perseus.

Dean, J. and J. Evans (1994), *Total Quality: management, organisation and strategy*, Minneapolis: West Publishing Company.

DeLamarter, R. (1988), *Big Blue: IBM's use and abuse of power*, London: Pan Books.

Denham, N., Ackers, P. and C. Travers (1997), 'Doing yourself out of a job? How middle managers cope with empowerment', *Employee Relations*, 19, pp. 147–159.

Department of Trade and Industry (1999), *Working for the Future: the changing face of work practices*, London: HMSO.

Dickson, T., McLachlan, H., Prior, P. and K. Swales (1988) 'Big Blue and the Unions: IBM, individualism and trade union strategy', *Work, Employment and Society*, 2 (4), pp. 506–520.

Eastman, C. and L. Fulop (1997), 'Management for clinicians or the case of "bringing the mountain to Mohammed"', *International Journal of Production Economics*, 52, pp. 15–30.

The Economist, (2001), 'A long march', 14th July, pp. 79–81.

Ehn, P. (1988), *Work-oriented Design of Computer Artifacts*, Stockholm: Arbetslivscentrum.

Eldridge, J.E.T. (1980), 'Space for sociology', *Sociology*, 14, pp. 94–103.

Emery, F. and E. Thorsrud, (1976), *Democracy at Work*, Leiden: Martinus Nijhoff.

Ennals, R. and B. Gustavsen (1999), *Work Organisation and Europe as a Development Coalition*, Amsterdam: John Benjamins.

European Commission (1997), *Partnership for a New Organisation of Work*, Green Paper, COM(97)128, Brussels: European Commission.

European Commission (1998), *Modernising the Organisation of Work: a positive approach to change*, COM(98)592, Brussels: European Commision.

European Foundation for the Improvement of Living and Working Conditions (1996) *Closing the Gap: direct participation in organisational change*, Luxembourg: Office for Official Publications of the European Communities.

Financial Times (2003), 'A speedier route from order to camcorder', 12th February, pp. 11.

Financial Times (2004), 'Chief executive pay soars 168% in five years', 24th May, p. 9.

Fincham, R. and P. Rhodes (1992), *The Individual, Work and Organization: behavioural studies for business and management*, Oxford: Oxford University Press.

Findlay, P., McKinlay, A., Marks, A. and P. Thompson (2000), 'Flexible when it suits them: the use and abuse of teamwork skills', in Procter, S. and F. Mueller (eds), *Teamworking*, Basingstoke: Macmillan, pp. 222–243.

Flanders, A. (1964), *The Fawley Productivity Agreements*, London: Faber.

Flowers, S. (1996), *Software Failure: management failure*, Chichester: Wiley.

Ford, H. and S. Crowther (1926), *My Life and Work*, New York: Doubleday.

Foster, D. and P. Hoggett (1999), 'Change in the benefits agency: empowering the exhausted worker', *Work, Employment and Society*, 13, pp. 19–39.

Fox, A. (1971), *The Sociology of Work in Industry*, London: Collier-Macmillan.

Foy, N. (1994), *Empowering People at Work*, Aldershot: Gower.

Geary, J. (1993), 'New forms of work organisation and employee involvement in two case study sites: plural, mixed and protean', *Economic and Industrial Democracy*, 14, pp. 511–534.

Geary, J. (1995), 'Work practices: the structure of work', in Edwards, P. (ed.) *Industrial Relations: theory and practice in Britain*, Oxford: Blackwell, pp. 368–396.

Giesekam, G. and S. Knight (2000), *Luvvies and Rude Mechanicals? Amateur and community theatre in Scotland*, Edinburgh: Scottish Arts Council.

Gill, C. and H. Krieger (2000), 'Recent survey evidence on participation in Europe: towards a European Model?', *European Journal of Industrial Relations*, 6 (1), pp. 109–132.

Gill, C., Gold, M. and P. Cressey (1999), 'Social Europe: national initiatives and responses', *Industrial Relations Journal*, 30 (4), pp.313–329.

Goffman, E. (1961) *Asylums: essays on the social situation of mental patients and other inmates*, London: Doubleday.

Goldthorpe, J., Lockwood, D., Bechofer, F. and J. Platt (1968), *The Affluent Worker: industrial attitudes and behaviour*, Cambridge: Cambridge University Press.

Goulding, D. and D. Currie (2000) (eds), *Thinking About Management: a reflective practice approach*, London: Routledge.

Graham, L. (1994), 'How does the Japanese model transfer to the United States? A view from the line', in Elger, T. and C. Smith (eds), *Global Japanisation? The transnational transformation of the labour process*, London: Routledge, pp. 123–151.

Greenbaum, J. and M. Kyng (1991) (eds) *Design at Work: co-operative design of computer systems*, Hillsdale, New Jersey: Lawrence Erlbaum.

Greene, A., Ackers, P. and J. Black (2001), 'Lost narratives? From paternalism to teamworking in a lock manufacturing firm', *Economic and Industrial Democracy*, 22 (2), pp.211–236.

Grey, C. (1994), 'Career as a project of the self and labour process discipline', *Sociology*, 28 (2), pp. 479–497.

The Guardian (1997a), 'Lost pay, lost time, lost expectations, lost trust', 11th July, p. 4.

The Guardian (1997b), 'Doctors sick of cabin crew rush', 11th July, p. 4.

Guest, D. (1997), 'Towards jobs and justice in Europe: a research agenda', *Industrial Relations Journal*, 28 (4), pp. 344–352.

Guidon, R. and B. Curtis (1988), 'Control of cognitive processes during design: what tools would support software designers?', Conference Proceedings of CHI, Washington DC, Chicago: ACM Press.

Gustavsen, B., Hofmaier, B., Ekman Philips, M. and A. Wikman (1996), *Concept-driven Development and the Organisation of the Process of Change: an evaluation of the Swedish Working Life Fund*, Amsterdam: John Benjamins.

Hagen, R., Miller S. and M. Johnson (2003), 'The disruptive consequences of introducing a critical management perspective onto an MBA programme', *Management Learning*, 34 (2), pp. 241–257.

Hales, C. (2000), 'Management and empowerment programmes', *Work, Employment and Society*, 14 (3), pp. 501–519.

Hall, M. and P. Marginson (2005), 'Trojan horses or paper tigers? Assessing the significance of European works councils', in Harley, B., Hyman, J. and P. Thompson (eds), *Participation and Democracy at Work: essays in honour of Harvie Ramsay*, Basingstoke: Palgrave Macmillan, pp. 204–221.

Hammer, M. and J. Champy (1993), *Reengineering the Corporation: a manifesto for business revolution*, London: Nicholas Brealey.

Harding, S. and G. Gilbert (1993), 'Negotiating the take up of formal methods', in Quintas, P. (ed.) *Social Dimensions of Systems Engineering: people, processes, policies and software development*, New York: Ellis Horwood.

Harley, B. (1999), 'The Myth of Empowerment: work organisation, hierarchy and employee autonomy in contemporary Australian workplaces', *Work, Employment and Society*, 13 (1), pp. 41–66.

Hatch, M. (1997), *Organisation Theory: modern, symbolic and postmodern perspectives*, Oxford: Oxford University Press.

Heller, F. (1999), 'Is participation really working?', *Quality of Working Life News and Abstracts*, 138, Spring, pp. 6–10.

Heller, F., Pusic, E., Strauss, G. and B. Wilpert (1998), *Organisational Participation: myth or reality*, Oxford: Oxford University Press.

The Herald (1996), 'Performance pay schemes backfire', 11th March, p. 5

The Herald (1997), 'Caterers' ballot turns up the heat on BA', 11th July, p. 2.

Herbert, S. (2004), *Arts in the Community, Scottish Parliament Information Centre Briefings*, Edinburgh: Scottish Executive.

Herzberg, F. (1968), 'One More Time: how do you motivate employees', *Harvard Business Review*, 46 (1), pp. 53–62.

Hindess, B. (1982), 'Power, interests and the outcomes of struggles', *Sociology,* 16 (4), pp. 498–511.

Hirschheim, R. and H. Klein (1994), 'Realizing emancipatory principles in information systems development: the case for ETHICS', *MIS Quarterly*, March, pp. 83–108.

Hofstede, G. (1991), *Cultures and Organisations: software of the mind*, London: McGraw-Hill.

Hopfl, H., Smith, S. and S. Spencer (1992), 'Values and valuations: corporate culture and job cuts', *Personnel Review*, 21 (1), pp. 24–38.

Howcroft, D. and M. Wilson (2003), 'Participation: 'bounded freedom' or hidden constraints on user involvement', *New Technology, Work and Employment*, 18 (1), pp. 2–19.

Hyman, R. (2005), 'Trade unions and the politics of the European social model', *Economic and Industrial Democracy*, 26 (1), pp. 9–40.

Ichniowski, C., Kochan, T., Levine, D., Olson, C. and G. Strauss (1996), 'What works at work: overview and assessment', *Industrial Relations*, 35 (3), pp. 299–333.

Jenkins, G. and M. Poole (1990) (eds), *New Forms of Ownership*, London: Routledge.

Johnson, D. and D. Redmond (1998), *The Art of Empowerment: the profit and pain of employee involvement*, London: Pitman.

Jones, O. (2000), 'Scientific management, culture and control: a first-hand account of Taylorism in practice', *Human Relations*, 53 (5), pp. 631–653.

Kanter, R. M. (1979), 'Power failure in management circuits', *Harvard Business Review*, 57 (4), pp. 65–75.

Kanter, R. M. (1984) *The Change Masters: corporate entrepreneurs at work*, London: Routledge.

Kelly, J. (1985), 'Managements redesign of work: labour process, labour markets and product markets', in Knights, D., Willmott, H. and D. Collinson (eds), *Job Redesign*, Aldershot: Gower, pp. 30–51.

Kenney, M. and R. Florida (1993), *Beyond Mass Production*, Oxford: Oxford University Press.

Khan, S. (1997), 'The key to being a leader company: empowerment', *Journal for Quality and Participation*, Jan-Feb, pp. 44–50.

Kraft, P. (1979), 'Challenging the Mumford democrats at Derby works', *Computing*, 2nd August, p. 17.

Labour Research Department (2002), 'Another year of executive excess', press release, 27th August.

Land, F. and R. Hirschheim (1983), 'Participative systems design: rationale, tools and techniques', *Journal of Applied Systems Analysis*, 10, p. 100.

Lecher, W., Platzer, H. Rub, S. and K. Weiner (2001), *European Works Councils: developments, types and networking*, Aldershot: Gower.

Littler, C. (1982), *The Development of the Labour Process in Capitalist Societies*, London: Heinemann.

Littler, C. (1985) (ed.), *The Experience of Work*, Aldershot: Gower.

Littler, C. and G. Salaman (1984), *Class at Work: the design, allocation and control of jobs*, London: Batsford.

Loveridge, R. (1980), 'What is participation? A review of the literature and some methodological problems', *British Journal of Industrial Relations*, 18 (3), pp. 297–317.

Lukes, S. (1974), *Power: a radical view*, London:Macmillan.

Mandel, E. (1973), 'The debate on workers' control', in Hunnius, G., Garson, G. and J. Case (eds), *Workers Control: a reader in labor and social change*, New York: Random House, pp. 344–373.

Marginson, P., Hall, M., Hoffmann, A. and T. Muller (2004), 'The impact of European works councils on management decision-making in UK and US-based multinationals: a case study comparison', *British Journal of Industrial Relations*, 42 (2), pp. 209–233.

Martin, R. and R. Fryer (1975), 'The deferential worker?', in Bulmer, M. (ed.), *Working Class Images of Society*, London: Routledge, pp. 98–115.

Martin, P. and J. Nicholls (1987), *Creating a Committed Workforce*, New York: McGrawHill.

McCabe, D. (2000), 'The team dream: the meaning and experience of teamworking for employees in an automobile manufacturing company', in Proctor, S. and F. Mueller (eds), *Teamworking*, Basingstoke: MacMillan, pp. 203–221.

McCabe, D. (2002), 'Waiting for dead men's shoes: towards a cultural understanding of management innovation', *Human Relations*, 55 (5), pp. 505–536.

McKinlay, A. and P. Taylor (1996), 'Power, surveillance and resistance: inside the factory of the future', in Ackers, P., Smith, C. and P. Smith (eds), *The New Workplace and Trade Unionism*, London: Routledge, pp. 279–300.

Michels, R. (1949), *Political Parties*, Glencoe: Free Press.

Miller, E. and A. Rice (1967), *Systems of Organisation: the control of task and sentient boundaries*, London: Tavistock.

Millward, N., Bryson, A. and J. Forth (2000), *All Change at Work? British Employment Relations 1980–1998, as Portrayed by the Workplace Industrial Relations Survey Series*, London: Routledge.

Mingers, J. (2000), 'What is it to be critical? Teaching a critical approach to management undergraduates', *Management Learning*, 31 (2), pp. 219–237.

Mitrofanov, S. (1966), *Scientific Principles of Group Technology*, Boston Spa: National Lending Library.

Moshavi, D. (2001), '"Yes and…": introducing improvisational theatre techniques to the management classroom', *Journal of Management Education*, 25 (4), pp. 437–449.

Mowshowitz, A. (1980), *Human Choice and Computers 2*, Amsterdam: North-Holland.

Mumford, E. (1979), 'The design of work: new approaches and new needs', in Rijnsdorp, J.E. (ed.), *Case Studies in Automation Related to the Humanisation of Work*, New York: Pergamon.

Mumford, E. (1980), 'The participative design of clerical information systems', in Bjorn-Andersen, N. (ed), *The Human Side of Information Processing*, Amsterdam: North-Holland.

Mumford, E. (1981), 'Participative systems design: structure and method', *Systems, Objectives, Solutions*, 1 (1), pp. 5–19.

Mumford, E. (1983), 'Successful systems design', in Otway, H. and M. Peltu (eds), *New Office Technology: human and organisational aspects*, London: Pinter, pp. 68–85.

Mumford, E. (1996), *Systems Design: ethical tools for ethical change*, London: Macmillan.

Mumford, E. and Cooper, C. (1979), *The Quality of Working Life in Western and Eastern Europe*, London: Associated Business Press.

Mumford, E. and R. Hendricks (1996), 'Business process re-engineering RIP', *People Management*, 2nd May, pp. 22–27.

Mumford, E. and D. Henshall (1979), *A Participative Approach to Computer Systems Design*, London: Associated Business Press.

Mumford, E. and B. MacDonald (1989), *XSEL's Progress: the continuing journey of an expert system*, London: Wiley.

Nardi, B. and J. Miller (1991), 'Twinkling lights and nested loops: distributed problem-solving and spreadsheet development', *International Journal of Man-Machine Studies*, 34, pp. 161–164.

Nicholls, J. (1995), 'Tackling hidden contempt', *People Management*, 30th November, p. 36.

Noon, M. and P. Blyton (1997), *The Realities of Work*, Basingstoke: Macmillan.

Nord, W. and J. Jermier (1992), 'Critical social science for managers? Promising and perverse possibilities', in Alvesson, M. and H. Willmott (eds), *Critical Management Studies*, London: Sage, pp. 202–222.

Oakland, J. (1996), *Total Quality Management: a practical approach*, European Centre for Total Quality Management, University of Bradford Management Centre.

O'Connell-Davidson, J. and T. Nichols (1991), 'Privatisation and employee share ownership: it's still us and them', *Financial Times*, 7th March, p. 21.

Ogbonna, E. and B. Wilkinson (1990), 'Corporate strategy and corporate culture: the view from the checkout', *Personnel Review*, 19 (4), pp. 9–15.

O'Reilly, N. (1995), 'Hero of the hour', *Personnel Today*, 9th May, p. 41.

Parker, M. and J. Slaughter (1988), *Choosing Sides: unions and the team concept*, Boston: South End Press.

Pascale, R. and A. Athos (1986), *The Art of Japanese Management*, London: Sidgwick and Jackson.

Pateman, C. (1970), *Participation and Democratic Theory*, Cambridge: Cambridge University Press.

Payne, J. and E. Keep (2005), 'Promoting workplace development: lessons for UK policy from Nordic approaches to job redesign and the Quality of Working Life', in Harley, B., Hyman, J. and P. Thompson (eds), *Participation and Democracy at Work: essays in honour of Harvie Ramsay*, Basingstoke: Palgrave Macmillan, pp. 146–165.

Pearson, A. (1988), *Primary Nursing: nursing in the Burford and Oxford nursing development units*, London: Chapman & Hall.

Pendleton, A. (1995), 'The impact of employee share ownership plans on employee participation and industrial democracy', *Human Resource Management Journal*, 5, pp. 44–60.

Peters, T. (1987), *Thriving on Chaos: handbook for a management revolution*, London: Macmillan.

Peters, T. and R. Waterman (1982), *In Search of Excellence: lessons from America's best-run companies*, New York: Harper and Row.

Pollard, C. W. (1996), *The Soul of the Firm*, Grand Rapids, Michigan: Zondervan Publishing House.

Pollert, A. (1996), 'Team work on the assembly line: contradiction and the dynamics of union resistance', in Ackers, P., Smith, C. and P. Smith (eds), *The New Workplace and Trade Unionism*, London: Routledge, pp. 178–210.

Poole, M. (1986), *Towards a New Industrial Democracy*, London: Routledge.

Poutsma, E., Hendrickx, J. and F. Huijgen (2003) 'Employee participation in Europe: in search of the participative workplace', *Economic and Industrial Democracy*, 24 (1), pp. 45–76.

Procter, S. and F. Mueller (2000) (eds), *Teamworking*, London: Macmillan.

Protherough, R. and J. Pick (2002), *Managing Britannia: culture and management in modern Britain*, Norfolk, England: Edgeways.

Qvale, T. (2002), 'A case of slow learning? Recent trends in social partnership in Norway with particular emphasis on workplace democracy', *Concepts and Transformation,* 7 (1), pp. 31–55.

Ramsay, H. (1977), 'Cycles of control: worker participation in sociological and historical perspective, *Sociology*, 11 (3), pp. 481–506.

Ramsay, H. (1980), 'Phantom participation: patterns of power and conflict', *Industrial Relations Journal*, 11 (3), pp. 46–58.

Ramsay, H. (1985), 'What is participation for? A critical evaluation of labour process analyses of job reform', in Knights, D., Willmott, H. and D. Collinson (eds), *Job Redesign: critical perspectives on the labour process*, Aldershot: Gower, pp. 52–80.

Ramsay, H. (1991), 'The community, the multinational, its workers and their charter: a modern tale of industrial democracy?', *Work, Employment and Society*, 5 (4), pp. 541–566.

Ramsay, H. (1993), 'Recycled waste? Debating the analysis of worker participation: a response to Ackers et al', *Industrial Relations Journal*, 24 (1), pp. 76–80.

Ramsay, H. (1997), 'Fools gold? European works councils and workplace democracy', *Industrial Relations Journal*, 28 (4), pp. 314–322.

Ramsay, H., Hyman, J., Baddon, L., Hunter, L. and J. Leopold (1990), 'Options for workers: owners or employees?', in Jenkins, G. and M. Poole (eds), *New Forms of Ownership: management and employment*, London: Routledge, pp. 183–204.

Randle, K. (1997), 'Rewarding failure: operating a performance-related pay system in pharmaceutical research', *Personnel Review*, 20 (3), pp. 187–200.

Ray, C. (1986), 'Corporate culture: the last frontier of control', *Journal of Management Studies*, 23, pp. 287–297.

Report of the Committee of Inquiry on Industrial Democracy (1977), Cmnd. 6706, Chairman: Lord Bullock, London: HMSO.

Robson, M. (1988), *The Journey to Excellence*, Wantage, England: MRA International.

Rosenbrock, H. (1990), *Machines with a Purpose*, Oxford, England: Oxford University Press.

Roth, W. (1997), 'Going all the way with empowerment', *The TQM Magazine*, 9, pp. 42–45.

Roy, D. (1969), 'Making out: a counter-system of workers' control of work situation and relationship', in T. Burns (ed.), *Industrial Man*, London: Penguin, pp. 359–379.

Roy, D. (1973), 'Banana time: job satisfaction and informal interaction', in Salaman, G. and K. Thompson (eds), *People and Organisations*, Harlow, England: Longman, pp. 205–222.

Salzman, H. and S. Rosenthal (1994), *Software by Design*, New York: Oxford University Press.

Sandberg, A. (1993), 'Volvo human centred work organisation: the end of the road?, *New Technology, Work and Employment*, 8 (2), pp. 83–87.

Sandberg, A. (1995), *Enriching production: perspectives on Volvo's Uddevalla plant as an alternative to lean production*, Aldershot: Avebury.

Sayles, L. (1958), *Behaviour of Industrial Work Groups*, London: Wiley.

Schein, E. (1985), *Organisational Culture and Leadership*, San Francisco: Jossey-Bass.

Schon, D. (1983), *The Reflective Practitioner*, Cambridge, Massachusetts: Basic Books.

Schuller, T. (1985), *Democracy at Work*, Oxford: Oxford University Press.

Scotland on Sunday (1999), 'Fat cats to be collared', 4th April, p. 5.

Semler, R. (1993), *Maverick: the success story behind the world's most unusual workplace*, London: Arrow.

Shaiken, H., Lopez, S. and I. Mankita (1997), 'Two routes to team production: Saturn and Chrysler compared', *Industrial Relations*, 36 (1), pp. 17–45.

Silver, J. (1987), 'The ideology of excellence: management and neoconservatism', *Studies in Political Economy*, 24, pp. 105–129.

Smith, S. and B. Wilkinson (1996), 'We are our own policemen: organising without conflict?', in Linstead, S., Grafton Small, R. and P. Jeffcutt (eds), *Understanding Management*, London: Sage, pp. 130–144.

Starkey, K. and A. McKinlay (1994), 'Managing for Ford', *Sociology*, 28, pp. 975–990.

Stirling, J. and B. Tully (2004), 'Power, process and practice: communications in European works councils', *European Journal of Industrial Relations*, 10 (1), pp. 73–89.

Storey, J. and K. Sisson (1993), *Managing Human Resources and Industrial Relations*, Milton Keynes: Open University Press.

Strauss, G. (1998), 'Participation works – if conditions are appropriate', in Heller, F., Pusic, E., Strauss, G. and B. Wilpert (eds), *Organisational Participation: myth or reality*, Oxford: Oxford University Press, pp. 190–219.

Sunday Telegraph (1993), 'Pay research shock for UK boardrooms', 26th September, p. 1.

Sward, K. (1948), *The Legend of Henry Ford*, New York: Rinehart.

Taylor, F. W. (1911), *The Principles of Scientific Management*, New York: W.W. Norton.

Thompson, P. (1986), 'Crawling from the wreckage: the labour process and the politics of production', proceedings of the Fourth Aston/UMIST Labour Process Conference, April.

Thompson, P. and P. Findlay (1996), 'The mystery of the missing subject', proceedings of the Fourteenth International Labour Process Conference, March.

Thompson, P. and D. McHugh (1995), *Work Organisation*, London: Macmillan.

Tracy, D. (1990), *10 Steps to Empowerment*, New York: Quill.

Trist, E. and K. Bamforth (1951), 'Some social and psychological consequences of the longwall method of coal getting', *Human Relations*, 4 (1), pp. 3–38.

Trist, E., Higgin, G., Murray, H. and A. Pollock (1963), *Organisational Choice: capabilities of groups at the coal face under changing technologies: the loss, rediscovery and transformation of a work tradition*, London: Tavistock.

Trist, E. and H. Murray (1993) (eds), *The Social Engagement of Social Science: a Tavistock anthology, vol. 2: the socio-technical perspective*, Philadephia: University of Pennsylvania Press.

Van Erven, E. (2001), *Community Theatre: global perspectives*, London: Routledge.

Waddington, J. (2003), 'What do representatives think of the practices of European works councils? Views from six countries', *European Journal of Industrial Relations*, 9 (3), pp. 303–325.

Ward, B. (1996), 'How to empower', *Canadian Manager*, Winter, pp. 20–22.

Watson, T. J. (1994), *In Search of Management: culture, chaos and control in managerial work*, London: Routledge.

Weizenbaum, J. (1976), *Computer Power and Human Reason: from judgement to calculation*, San Francisco: Freeman.

Wickens, P. (1993), 'Steering the middle road to car production', *Personnel Management*, June, pp. 34–38.

Wilkinson, A. (1998), 'Empowerment: theory and practice', *Personnel Review*, 27 (1), pp. 40–56.

Willmott, H. (1993), 'Strength is ignorance; slavery is freedom: managing culture in modern organisations', *Journal of Management Studies*, 30 (5), pp. 515–552.

Wills, J. (1999), 'European works councils in British firms', *Human Resource Management Journal*, 9 (4), pp. 19–38.

Wilson, D., Petocz, P. and K. Roiter (1996), 'Software quality assurance in practice', *Software Quality Journal*, 5, pp. 53–59.

Womack, J., Jones, D. and D. Roos (1990), *The Machine that Changed the World: the triumph of lean production*, New York: Rawson Macmillan.

Wong, E. and G. Tate (1994), 'A study of user participation in information systems development', *Journal of Information Technology*, 9, pp. 51–60.

Wood, S. (1999), 'The British General Election of 1997', *Electoral Studies*, 18 (1), pp. 142–147.

Wright, M. and P. Edwards (1998), 'Does teamworking work, and if so, why? A case study in the aluminium industry', *Economic and Industrial Democracy*, 19 (1), pp. 59–90.

Wright-Mills, C. (1973), *The Sociological Imagination*, Harmondsworth, Middlesex: Pelican.

Yates, C., Lewchuk, W. and P. Stewart (2001), 'Empowerment as a Trojan horse: new systems of work organisation in the North Amercian automobile industry', *Economic and Industrial Democracy*, 22, pp. 517–541.

Yeates, D., Shields, M. and D. Helmy (1994), *Systems Analysis and Design*, London: Pitman.

Young, E. (1989), 'On the naming of the rose: interests and multiple meanings as elements of organisational culture', *Organization Studies*, 10 (2), pp. 187-206.

Index